*A Capernaum Story*

by Nick Palermo

Goehner Publications
San Jose, Calif.

*Missing Stars, Fallen Sparrows*
*A Capernaum Story*
by Nick Palermo

Printed in the United States of America

ISBN 9781628393170

www.xulonpress.com

Nick Palermo is more than just the founder of Capernaum, a ministry to kids with disabilities in Young Life. He is the epicenter of a movement spreading across the globe. *Missing Stars, Fallen Sparrows* gives you a front-row seat to see and feel this incredible story. No one tells it better than Nick and no one has lived this story more than Nick. It's the story of God's passionate pursuit of precious kids He loves - kids who are changing our lives, one by one. Read this book and get copies for all your friends. Our world needs this good news.

**Denny Rydberg,** *President*
*Young Life*

≈

This book opens the door to what the life of a person with a disability is really like. It shows how Young Life Capernaum improves the quality of a disabled person's life by exploring God and who He is through adventures. How do I know? Because I was a Club kid and Nick Palermo was my Club leader! His 27 years of experience and down-to-earth manner let him talk about God in a way that is easy for young people with disabilities to understand. Read this book and open the door to a world you might not know much about.

**Adan Bustos,** *Leader (and former Club kid)*
*Capernaum*

≈

> WARNING - Reading this book will cause your heart to be broken and your eyes to be opened to the opportunity for ministry with the disabled.

Ministry leaders and pastors: You need to read this book! If you don't read *Missing Stars, Fallen Sparrows* for the ministry opportunities it presents, read it to experience the kingdom of God in all its fullness. Nick Palermo tells how his friends with disabilities showed him the way of Jesus and the heart of God.

> **Paul Bertelson**, *Founder*
> *Real Resources (YouthWorks, Youth Specialties,*
> *The Table Project and BigStuf Camps)*

~

God caused Nick Palermo to begin a ministry within Young Life that is beautifully consistent with this mission's history and commitment. Capernaum Ministries is pure incarnational witness. These wonderful - and oftentimes overlooked - young people with disabilities need to hear about Jesus (as do able-bodied kids), and Nick led the way to see that it could happen.

> **Bob Mitchell**, *Former President*
> *Young Life*

~

As a grandfather of a child with Down syndrome, I'm grateful for Capernaum. Without Nick Palermo, thousands of kids like my granddaughter wouldn't be blessed though this ministry. Read this book, but beware! The stories will inspire and change you. Forever.

> **Ted Johnson,** *Senior Vice President*
> *Young Life*

# Contents

# Foreword

Years ago, while staying at a camp, I met a fabulous couple from Oregon and we ended up hanging out together for the week. They were joyful, vibrant and seemed to have it all together as they talked about their vacations, boating adventures, and the achievements of their children.

As I got to know them a little more I noticed that they talked often of their youngest daughter. She was a shining point in their lives, but not the central point. They described her as delightful, funny, musical, effervescent and having multiple disabilities, including moderate mental retardation.

Two stories from their lives stood out to me. The first was their recollection of the conversations they had before each of their four children were born. These conversations centered around their commitment that Christ - not the baby, and eventually, the child - would be the center of their lives. Their commitment was to one another and to their family, and applied equally to their youngest, even after her disability diagnoses. Both parents told me their commitments to God, to each other and to their kids saved their marriage, even their very lives.

The second story they told will grab the attention of any youth worker. The church in which they were active urged 12 to 18 year olds to join a small group (with a consistent leader) that would stick together from the 7th through 12th grades. When their youngest daughter joined it was the highlight of her week.

By 9th grade, however, her parents recognized that she was distancing from her peers in abilities and social skills. Mom quietly approached the leader, asking for her help to begin transitioning her daughter out of the group so she would not be a distraction or disrupt the spiritual growth of the other girls.

The leader flatly refused. "Your daughter is an integral part of who we are as a group! The rest of the girls in the group need her just as much as she needs them."

My friends' daughter was not a problem. She was a friend who was gifted at teaching compassion, attentiveness and patience. A few of the other girls heard of the mother's concerns and wrote, letting the parents know how grateful they were for trusting their daughter's friendship to a bunch of squirrely girls who were trying to figure life out.

"*Missing Stars, Fallen Sparrows*" has dozens of stories like this, stories from the life of Nick Palermo, a guy who's still trying to figure it all out. Some of the stories you'll read don't have what most would consider happy endings, but they are a very real part of the journey of following Christ as He invites the crippled, the blind, and the lame to His banquet table.

I'd suggest picking one of two ways to get the most out of this book. The first: Get into some comfy clothes, find a cozy blanket and a large cup of tea, and read the stories from cover to cover. You may feel like you're sitting in Nick Palermo's living room as he pours out his heart through story after story, while his wife, Sue, offers unending hospitality.

Don't look for a chronological or sequential thread to the stories; it's there, but not in the ways you might expect. Instead, listen with your heart to the joys and celebrations, as well as the heartbreaks and struggles. Both are equally important parts of this yet-unfinished narrative God is writing in the world of ministry and disability.

The other way to read this book is over time, with a pen and paper (or your favorite electronic device) nearby so you can capture your thoughts and responses. Read it slowly, asking questions as Nick shares the stories. Write down your questions and prayers to God as you immerse yourself in the lives of these special friends.

Reflect after each section with pointed honesty and humility. Whether you choose to read a chapter a day or a chapter a week, don't rush. Let the words sink in and marinate your own heart and mind. Allow the Holy Spirit to speak through the words on the pages. Nick's heart for you as you read is that you hear the voices of his friends. The compelling voices and stories of these who are Christ's friends!

If you have ever had the pleasure of meeting Nick, you know that he is a baseball-loving, family-devoted, slightly hyperactive, short, loud man; a mysterious mix of magnetism and humility. He is the first to tell you about his faults and believes that while he has something to offer, Jesus has so much more. He has been with and listened to friends with disabilities for three decades, but Nick Palermo is not the person he is hoping you'll get to know. It is Jesus Christ, first of all, and second, his friends with disabilities.

This is a book for anyone who is open to including those with disabilities in their ministry. The church and ministry communities need to hear these voices and understand that we are incomplete without them. To truly be imitators of Christ as beloved children, we must include all His children.

I once asked parents of teens with disabilities what they wished others knew about their kids. Here is what one mother said:

*"I wish other people knew that these kids have feelings, that they deserve the right to be heard, that time is important to them. I really wish there was a bigger place for them in church. Even the events they do with other church groups don't include any activities for the kids with special needs. That would be one of my biggest things; I really wish the*

*church would get more involved. It's not easy - I realize that more than you know - but if we can put so much effort and strength into creating other opportunities for kids, why not this?"*

In these pages, Nick not only tells us his answer to this mom's wish, but talks about the dreams of others who have sensed this same call from God: to truly know our friends with disabilities. It is still a work in progress.

As you read, get ready to be challenged, blessed and, just maybe, encouraged into beginning some of the most-rewarding relationships you'll ever know.

**Amy Jacober,** PhD, MSW

# Preface

It was 1971. I was a very lonely and lost teenager, struggling through my junior year in high school. Thankfully, the Young Life leaders at my school, Johnie and Jane Thomsen and Carol Kerley, came into my life. They not only cared about me, they lived out their faith and told me about Jesus Christ in ways that changed my life forever and charted my future. After high school I became a Young Life leader and eventually joined the full-time staff, reaching out to love-needy high school kids, just like my leaders had loved me.

In the fall of 1980 - totally and unexpectedly - I met my first young friends with physical and intellectual disabilities. Once again, my life was changed forever.

2012 marked my 40th year in youth ministry with Young Life. For more than 30 of those years, my young friends have been writing their stories on the pages of my heart. The result is the book they themselves could not write, but you can now read. They have given me profound truths and life-changing perspectives, even though they cannot voice what they're teaching me! Most around them - including Christians - neither receive nor hear them.

I wrote this book because I want you to meet my friends! I want you to hear their voices and know their stories. I want the Christian community to discover these missing stars and fallen sparrows, precious not only to God but to me and thousands of others, too.

In Isaiah 40:26 we read, *"Lift up your eyes and look to the heavens: Who created all these? He who brings out the starry host one by one and calls forth each of them by name, Because of His great power and mighty strength, **not one of them is missing**."*

In Matthew 10:29 Jesus tells us, *"Are not two sparrows sold for a penny? Yet not one of them falls to the ground apart from the will of your Father."*

God tracks each of the trillions of stars and not one goes missing. But kids with disabilities are missing from our churches (though not from God's love and care).

An ordinary fallen sparrow on the roadside is ignored and passed by, but the Heavenly Father notices. Tragically, most people in our churches walk right by the kids with disabilities, those who God holds as treasured jewels.

I've written this book because my life has been lit up by the beautiful stars and lovely, simple sparrows that grabbed my attention. The ones who taught me to fly. May I introduce them to you?

**Nick Palermo**
December 2012

# Acknowledgements

*"God made man because He loves stories."*

That's my favorite quote. It's from Holocaust survivor Elie Wiesel who waited silently for 15 years before writing "Night," the award-winning chronicle of that terrible time.

Writing the stories in this book has made me realize more than ever that many, many people have written into my life. Among the hundreds who have formed my story, I want to thank and honor a few:

My life partner, Susie, and my three amazing sons - Joel, Zack, and Sam - who support and cheer me on.

My Young Life leaders, Johnie and Jane Thomsen. They loved me to Christ, setting me on a course, a mission to love kids the rest of my life.

Mary Ann Vollrath, who believed in me when no one else did. She fought to keep me on staff and appointed me as Young Life's first staff person for kids with disabilities.

Desirree Madison-Biggs, who helped me with my first attempt at a manuscript.

Clif Davidson, my supervisor for 18 years, who fought for starting and continuing Capernaum when it was not embraced.

Bob Mitchell and Les Comee, who gave me the freedom and encouraged my heart to attempt this new Young Life ministry.

Amy Jacober, my Deborah (from the book of Judges), who opened up so many new arenas for me.

Lydia Martinez, who relentlessly prayed and pushed me to write. I feel like she birthed this book.

Dave Martinez and his constant encouragement.

My birth and adoptive families, which love and support me in all I do.

Everyone who has contributed prayerfully and financially to the publication of this book.

Don Goehner, Steve Van Atta and Kathy Skye – the team that made this book a reality. Steve, you taught me so much about writing. See you at Harry's Hofbrau!

Every Capernaum kid. Each of you has changed my life.

Capernaum staff, volunteers, committee members and donors, who have made my life forever richer and better.

My new ministry team, with whom I will create even more stories: Shelley Smith, Kristie Morrison, Pete Cantu, Otila Salazar Torres, Helen Lallo, Lee Jarmillo, Manuel Torres, Joel Palermo and Jessica Thompson.

Steve and Cathy Chung, who are constantly by my side.

Jen Exsted, for her constant presence in my life.

Alberto and Bernie, best friends for many years who open doors for me and stand by me in adversity.

My friend Melody, who brings music into my life.

Ted Johnson, the greatest encourager I've ever known.

Ken and Alice Kerley and Carol Kerley, Joe and Elie Kerley, a beloved family who made this ministry possible.

Bill Younger and his family, John Mumford, Walter Hansen, and Floyd and Jean Kvamme, who have helped this ministry travel around the world.

Donna Hatasaki, who has always inspired me with her writing.

Pam, Amira, Lyn, John, Suzanne, and John, my partners in this beautiful story that continues to be written.

Alan Smyth and Scott Lisea, the guys I would choose to be stranded on an island with!

Shelley, who has taken the torch from me and made it even brighter.

Cindy Carter and K.C. Yatsko, who saved my life early on, and sent me healed into my future.

My beautiful mother, whom I met when I was 24, who made my life complete the moment I looked upon her face.

Finally and most importantly, my Prince of Peace, Jesus Christ, who wrote me into His Book of Life.

# Introduction

Thank you for opening this book. It is for anyone who has ever been uncomfortable around a person with a disability, especially my fellow youth ministers who live among young people so faithfully and lovingly in the name of Jesus. Your passion is to love every kind of kid, including kids with disabilities.

This book is for you.

In the pages that follow, I've tried to anticipate your questions - the same questions I've asked and continue to ask - about how to effectively reach and love these special kids:

- How do I include them?
- How do I get beyond my own fears and discomfort?
- How do I help my able-bodied kids engage with them?
- How can I do this work, when I'm already feeling overwhelmed?

Starting 30 years ago, God set me on a journey with a very steep learning curve. He used my treasured friends with disabilities to teach me and, if you're willing, the friends in your life can teach you, too. You don't need a PhD or extensive experience in this kind of ministry to start including kids with disabilities in your life. You simply need the desire to be a friend and learn from these new friends.

As you read and meet my friends I pray that you will find yourself desiring to look for and find kids with disabilities in the neighborhoods, schools, and churches near you. When these missing stars and fallen sparrows you find begin to be known by name and start receiving your care, you will be blessed beyond anything you've ever experienced!

As you read and have questions, jot them down. I'd love to dialogue with you or, maybe, you could visit Capernaum in San Jose. Feel free to use the contact information on Page 154 to get in touch.

Can I pray with you as we begin?

*Jesus, lover of the least, thank You for this new friend who picked up this book. I pray they will be encouraged as they read about how You love the less-than-cool people. I pray hard that everyone who reads this book will become intimate friends with one child with a disability and their family this coming year. When that happens, Lord God, I know You will forever and lovingly wreck this reader's life for good! I pray they will fall in love with the kids the world has rejected, but You have selected. Amen.*

Be encouraged!

# A Word to the Reader

I pray that each page you read will make you feel welcome and drawn into the world of my friends with disabilities. As we journey together into that world, let me provide you with some background information, much of it from my personal ministry in Young Life.

The name of our ministry, Capernaum, is taken from Jesus' encounter with a paralyzed man in the town of Capernaum. I chose that name because everything in that Gospel story captures what we experience with our friends with disabilities.

You'll find me referring to our "Clubs," Young Life's weekly outreach to non-Christian kids. (You could just as easily substitute "youth group" for "Club.")

"Campaigners" is our small-group Bible study for kids who have committed their lives to Christ and want to learn what it means to follow Jesus.

"Contact work" is spending time with kids on their turf and schedule, in order to build deep, lasting, unconditional friendships.

With 23 Young Life camp properties across the nation, camping is a huge piece of our ministry. When I refer to "camp" or "camping," it is usually at one of our Young Life locations where kids go for a week or a weekend, experiencing the proclamation of the Gospel in word and deed.

I hope and pray you can apply the heart and ministry tools from these stories into your day-to-day experience with your youth group and students. I pray that reading this book will change your thinking about the value and the practical aspects of including young people with disabilities in your life and ministry.

You are one of my heroes. Why? Because of the great job you are doing as you love students. Thank you for your love, hard work and commitment to youth who desperately need the hope of Jesus in this broken world.

God bless you as you read!

# Dedication

To my big brother, Gene, who taught me baseball and life.
I love you and miss you, every day!

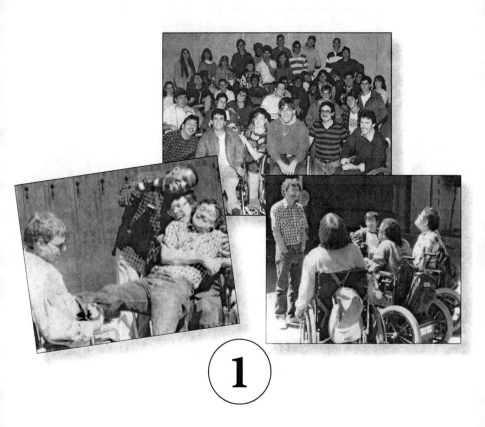

$\left(\begin{array}{c} \mathbf{1} \end{array}\right)$

# It Began With Steve

*Our journey begins on a sunny fall day in 1980*
*when I met 25 of the 600 million people with*
*disabilities and found my life unexpectedly changed.*

~

*"If you really want to make God laugh,
tell Him your plans."*

- C. S. LEWIS

~

After graduating from high school in 1972, I became a volunteer Young Life leader. Each week I spent hours on high school campuses, loving on kids and trying my best to be the good news of Christ to them, just like my Young Life leader did for me. Nothing else mattered to me. I loved Jesus and I wanted my high school friends to know Him.

Back to that fall day in 1980. I was going to the Blackford High School campus as a new leader for that school. Blackford was one of 35 high schools in San Jose, Calif., the 10th largest city in the United States. Up to 20 percent of San Jose's 52,000 high school students have some form of disability, matching the national average. I called up one of the leaders that morning and asked him to take me to Blackford so I could meet kids at lunch, as I had been doing at other schools for the previous eight years. That was my plan, anyway.

But as C. S. Lewis said, "If you really want to make God laugh, tell Him your plans."

My friend David and I drove to the school. We prayed for our time with kids and then sauntered over to the inner campus, arriving about 10 minutes before lunch began. As we turned the corner, 25 kids in motorized wheelchairs sped straight toward us, before taking sharp right turns into the cafeteria. I thought I was at the Indianapolis 500! I had never seen students in wheelchairs on any high-school campus, traveling together in a pack.

I recovered my composure and asked Dave, "Who are those kids?" He replied, "I don't know. I've never seen them." It was years later that I remembered this comment from my dear friend and fellow Young Life leader. A comment reflecting a reality that was – and still is – both sad and widespread.

Dave had been a leader at Blackford for three years, but had never noticed these kids. Like Dave, most people in our culture are unaware of kids with disabilities. These kids are marginalized because, at a time of their lives when it is crucial for them to feel like they fit in, they stand out as misfits. Their appearance, slurred speech, disfigurement and intellectual disabilities make them a threat to their peers. Administrators and teachers are often ill-equipped to meet the classroom needs of kids with disabilities, and don't welcome the added work and distraction that they add to the school day. They are ignored, often without prejudice or ill intention, but ignored nonetheless.

When I said, "Dave, come on, let's go meet these kids," you need to know I had no background with people with disabilities personally or professionally. I knew nothing, but in that Christopher-Columbus moment of discovery, I entered a new world I didn't even know existed.

We walked through the cafeteria doors and I strode up to the first kid I saw. I am confident and an extrovert, so I really didn't think I had any fears. But that quickly changed.

It all started with Steve. After hearing someone calling out his name, I quickly and innocently said, "Hi, Steve," and put my hand out to shake his. He said something, but his speech was so garbled I couldn't understand a word. Then he reached out his hand to shake mine and I shuddered. His hand was gnarled, like the bark of an old oak tree. I was shocked and didn't know what to do. I quickly withdrew my hand and said, "Nice meeting you." As another kid with slurred speech said something to me I panicked. "Oh God," I thought, "what is he saying? And what am I doing here??"

Then, a girl in a wheelchair next to me dropped her pencil on the floor. I instinctively went to pick it up and she drooled on my arm. That did it! Frozen by embarrassment and way beyond anything resembling my comfort zone, I quickly left the cafeteria (without the confidence I had carried into that room).

But, you know what? I couldn't stop thinking about those kids. Over the next month I continued spending time on campus with these students, trying to connect with them. I sweated, not knowing what to do or say. I was speechless most of the time (which my friends would consider a miracle along the lines of the Virgin birth), but kept returning anyway. Time after time I entered their world feeling awkward and left feeling, well, awkward.

But I wasn't giving up. Not after what God had done in my life. Nine years before that first encounter at Blackford High School, Jesus Christ grabbed hold of my life at a Young Life camp called Woodleaf. While there, I listened to the greatest news I'd ever heard. The God of the universe put on flesh and blood and visited our planet. He – Jesus – came to invite me to know Him.

My heart was pumping so loud I thought every one of the 300 kids in that room could hear it, but I didn't care! I said, "Jesus I want to follow You." And, within months of starting to follow Jesus, I knew I wanted to be a Young Life leader. More than that, I told God and my area director I wanted to be part of the Young Life staff, like my leader, Johnie Thomsen. I thought God was behind my candidacy, but my area director wasn't convinced. "That's nice, Nick. Call me in five or six years."

But God was up to something and one morning, He let me in on what He had in store for me: Something very new and different.

It happened one morning while reading the Gospel of Luke. Luke is my favorite Gospel because, during my senior year in high school I met my Young Life leader, Johnie, every Friday morning at 6:15 for hot chocolate, doughnuts, and Luke.

A kid like me should never have been given that much sugar, but my Young Life leader was brave and he heaped up a serving of

Luke every Friday morning that made me fall even more deeply in love with Jesus.

Years later, I was reading a very familiar passage from my beloved Gospel. One morning, a month after meeting kids with disabilities, I read this:

"Then Jesus said to him, 'Someone gave a great dinner and invited many. At the time for the dinner he sent his slave to say to those who had been invited, "Come, for everything is ready now."

"But they all began to make excuses. The first said to him, "I have bought a piece of land and I must go out and see it. Please accept my apologies." 'Another said, "I have just been married and therefore I cannot come." 'So the slave returned and reported this to his master.'

"Then the owner of the house became angry and said to his slave, "Go out at once into the streets and lanes of the town and bring in the poor, the crippled, the blind, the lame."' (Luke14:16-21)

The last sentence hit me like a baseball line drive to my forehead. For the second time in a month my world was upended - this time by Jesus through the words of Luke.

The poor! The crippled! The blind! The lame! As I read these words it dawned on me that in all the years I had read this passage, heard it preached and discussed it in Bible studies, it had been explained as a story about the spiritually poor, the spiritually lame, the spiritually blind, and the spiritually crippled.

But after reading in Luke 14, all I could think about were the kids in wheelchairs in that high school cafeteria who had rolled into my heart. They were really and truly poor, lame, blind and crippled. Their disabilities were actual, not just spiritual. I had missed the heart of Jesus' message, I think, because we Christians tend to spiritualize things that have a solid physical reality. We often make the mistake of interpreting and re-interpreting when the literal, simple, complete truth is right in front of us.

I was shocked at how I had misread this passage. Jesus was talking about actual people with straight-up physical and intellectual disabilities. How had I missed this? How had every Christian I had ever known missed this? My confusion and chaos were interrupted by Jesus' familiar-yet-inaudible whisper: "Nick, *be comfortable with being uncomfortable*." I chuckled nervously, trying to convince myself I could get used to being comfortable with being uncomfortable sometime in the future. (More on that in the next chapter.)

As I had done dozens of times before, I got into my car, drove to Blackford High and entered the cafeteria. But this time was different. Walking in and probably looking like I was in need of medical attention, I repeated to myself over and over, "*Be comfortable with being uncomfortable. Be comfortable with being uncomfortable.*"

Thirty-year-old non-teaching, non-staff adults are already out of place on a high school campus, but when they walk around talking to themselves, their status drops to a sub-freshman level. Even if I looked weird and didn't feel very cool, I knew there was no other place in the world I was supposed to be at that moment.

I walked over to the kid who was the hardest to understand. You guessed it: Steve. He had been trying to talk to me the entire month and I had pretended to understand him the entire month. Nevertheless, Steve wouldn't stop trying to communicate with me. This time I would not run away.

"Steve, would you repeat that? I really want to understand." "*Be comfortable with being uncomfortable. Be comfortable with being uncomfortable,*" I said to myself under my breath. Steve tried again. Nope, I couldn't get what he was saying. I asked Steve to try again. After the fourth or fifth try, I was getting red faced and embarrassed.

Then God sent an interpreter. Steve's friend, Caesar (who spoke clearly), sat down next to him and told me, "Nick, he just said he's glad you're here today." A momentary silence, and then the three of us busted out laughing. With each laugh, the tension of the past month dropped off like bricks falling out of my soul.

It was in that moment that Steve and his friends became to me kids who happened to have disabilities, instead of disabilities who happened to be kids. The difference in perception is like the 10-mile gap between the south rim of the Grand Canyon and its north rim. Steve became more than a kid. He became one in a long line of high schoolers who became my friends. I began to see Steve, the person created by God, not Steve the disability.

"How did this happen?" I wondered as I left the cafeteria. Soon, my wondering became a prayer of thanksgiving.

"God, in Your wisdom, You had me arrive early to my high school campus one fall day. You did this so I would see kids (with disabilities) I had never seen before. I entered their world in the cafeteria and walked out terrified and embarrassed."

But, every time I went back to the campus I saw these kids and felt the Holy Spirit urge me to connect with them. God used His Word to open my eyes in a new way to Luke 14. I finally read it right and heard God whisper, "*Be comfortable with being uncomfortable.*" With each trip back to the cafeteria my conviction grew stronger: These kids were going to become my friends and be part of who I am, for the rest of my life.

By then my response to God was pretty straightforward. "I give up. I'm in!"

Back in my car I said to God, "I can't wait until tomorrow! I'm ready to keep on being comfortable with being uncomfortable!" I had much to learn as I entered the world of kids with disabilities, but I started small with that simple phrase, *"Be comfortable with being uncomfortable."* Those words got me through many new and awkward moments as I learned how to be a good friend to teens with disabilities.

**Consider:** What do you fear when you're around someone with a disability?

## 2

# Be Comfortable With Being Uncomfortable

*After the Lord whispered those words to me and I began
living them out, it was like finally finding the right key to
unlock a door that seemed impenetrable.*

~

*The crazy, unexpected and sad thing is that we*
*– the able-bodied and fully functioning ones who are*
*supposedly disability-free –*
*are the ones who are so uncomfortable.*
*Not only around kids with disabilities but,*
*tragically, with ourselves.*

~

After the Lord whispered those words to me and I began living them out, it was like finally finding the right key to unlock a door that seemed impenetrable. It was the key to facing my fears head on and refusing to run from them. God's direction to me was the key to taking a deep breath and leaning into something very difficult, but knowing He had my back.

When that key turned the tumblers and the door slowly opened, the first thing I encountered was a room filled with laughter and the promise of friendship. As it turned out, only the door was imposing and forbidding. We make assumptions about closed doors and what we'll find on the other side of them. The scarier the door looks, the easier it is to run from it.

Strangely, what I found out as I opened the "Be Comfortable with Being Uncomfortable" door was a room full of new friends with physical and intellectual disabilities who were, actually, very comfortable with themselves. Most of them had been living with their disabilities since birth, so they were used to being shunned and denied opportunities their able-bodied peers took for granted.

After Jesus gave me the key to that door and I began including my friends with disabilities in my life, it was easy to forget that I had been so uncomfortable around them. Now, that's not to say I don't still get uncomfortable as I meet kids, but now I am comfortable with that familiar feeling. Kids who are comfortable in their own skin make me comfortable.

Let me tell you about a kid I met who is more comfortable with himself than any kid I've ever met. His name is Adán (pronounced a-don, with a short a and a short o sound).

I met Adán 21 years ago, when he was 10 years old and attending Rogers Middle School. Adán is of Mexican descent and has cerebral palsy. He speaks clearly and has a quick wit, a sly smile and a wild, go-for-it attitude. "Hell on wheels" would have been a good way to describe him then.

I had just started a Capernaum Club at Adán's school and was visiting with new kids one fall day in 1990. As I walked into the middle of the campus at lunch I spotted two kids in wheelchairs running their chairs full speed off a curb of increasing heights. I looked on in disbelief at these two crazy kids. But I had to meet them!

So, I approached the first kid and said, "Hi, I'm Nick. What's your name?" He gave me a "Who-the-?!&$-are-you?" look and uttered the first words of our not-yet-begun friendship: "Will you take me to an X-rated movie?" I tried to keep from laughing as I replied, "Let me think about that for a second... No!!" But our friendship was on its way and Adán and his friend, Keith, signed up for Club.

Years later, he told me he came because he had nothing else to do and was bored. (A lot of kids with disabilities face a seemingly unending series of boring days and nights.) Adan wanted to do everything everyone else wanted to do, but he didn't have the opportunities or transportation to get there. Before, he hardly ever left his home after school, but now, with Club, he had someplace to go. He wanted to hear more. At first, I think he just came to mock me, but when he heard me talking about how God doesn't make mistakes and how He has a purpose for everyone, including him, well, that got his attention.

His first Club was epic and extreme, which are good words to describe Adán. One kid was hit in the face with a pie, causing him to scream out that he wanted to be pied 30 times. So, wanting to fully earn his trust, he got 30 pies in his face.

That afternoon's Club talk was about Jesus on the sea, calming the storm. In the middle of the talk, Adán yelled out, "That's bulls___!" In all the years of leading Club and giving Club talks I had never heard a kid say out loud what a number of the kids might have thought. Not Adán. As he has said many times, "I have no problem telling you when and where you should go."

We fought for the next four years. He was loud, vulgar and angry. His mother was a single parent who spoke only Spanish. His father had left them and Adán was intensely bitter toward him.

He was also angry at being in a wheelchair. Often, when kids teased and taunted him, Adán, never one to back down, would start fighting them. He was in the principal's office as often as he was in the classroom. (Years later, when Adán was a Club leader at the same middle school he attended, he took a new leader out to campus to meet kids. Entering the school office, Adán casually said, "This is where I spent most of my time.")

When we went to camp together for the first time, Adán tested me all week long. But he had the greatest week of his life. Besides trying to talk to every girl at camp, he challenged the entire camp to mud-wrestle him. Seventy-five kids showed up and Adán took them on in the mud for three hours. Sixteen years later, he tells me, he is still finding mud on his body in strange places.

At the end of the week I asked him what he thought about what he had heard about Jesus. His matter-of-fact reply: "I liked it, but Jesus is for white people." When I told him that Jesus was probably brown-skinned, he stared at me in disbelief and then said, "No way, man. You are b.s.-ing me."

I took him and his best friend to camp again a year later. This time, it all clicked for both of them and they gave their lives to Christ. They rolled out of the Club room screaming, "We are Gospel gangsters!"

From that day forward I saw an amazing change in Adán. His anger slowly left. He began to take a real interest in the lives of others, including mine. He began treating others with respect. He had hope. For the first time ever, he belonged. But two things did not change; his passion and self-assurance.

I took him backpacking, mountain climbing and rappelling – all with him in his wheelchair. I watched him climb a 75-foot incline unassisted, using only his arms. An ascent most people would've done in 10 minutes took him an hour. The guides kept saying, "You can stop, Adán. You've already done a great job! Look at how far you've gone!!" Adán's screaming response surprised no one. "No, I've got to do this. For God!"

He just wouldn't give up. When he got to the top, trembling from the exertion, he yelled repeatedly, "I did it for God! I did it for God!" We all cried, completely blown away by Adán's powerful faith and his incredible resolve.

Here was a kid who had become precious to me since he'd first stormed into my life. While most pitied him, he wasn't in that group. He was good with how God had created him. He believed in himself, causing those of us around him to do so, too.

At one of our large events, Adán challenged three of his Mexican friends to a salsa-eating contest. (The salsa, of course, was hot enough to burn through steel.) Each kid took a chip and loaded it up with salsa and ate it, repeating the routine until all but one contestant was still eating. Two rounds passed and Adán became impatient. He grabbed the jar from me and quickly gulped down the whole jar. With nova-star heat causing his eyes to weep, he took his shirt off and in his best Mohammed Ali shout declared, "I'm so pretty. Can't nobody beat me." Standing ovation, contest over.

As I had during his solo climb and numerous other times, I watched in stunned wonder. The whole jar of fiery salsa! Why?

Because he lives comfortably with a red-hot passion for life; he loves to win; and he doesn't care what anyone thinks.

Adán is now 31 years old and is one of my very best friends. No one, and I mean no one, makes me laugh as often and as hard as he does. He is loyal and full of life. He is a Capernaum leader and he tells kids, "I am glad God made me this way. You should be too, because He can do great things with us just the way we are!"

Adán lives each day with a new perspective on his life. He knows he is not a mistake, and that he serves the God who specializes in using flawed, imperfect, awesome people. He knows God's power is perfected in our weakness.

The crazy, unexpected and sad thing is that **we** – the able-bodied and fully functioning ones who are supposedly disability-free – are the ones who are so uncomfortable. Not only around kids with disabilities but, tragically, with ourselves.

Adán and his friends are my mentors in self-acceptance. They help me to be comfortable with being uncomfortable - with them, myself, and everyone else I meet.

So, grab hold of Jesus' key to wholeness and walk through that door into the life of a person with a disability. Take a risk. Leave your comfort zone. If and when you do, you will find your life transformed and changed forever as you see yourself - and God - more clearly through the life of a person with a disability.

**Consider:** This week, try to meet and get to know someone with a disability.

$$3$$

# Turn Me

*"Come on gang! Let's blow this popsicle stand!" I yelled at
the top of my lungs. Nine of my new friends in wheelchairs and eight
leaders were heading to our first weekend camp together at Young Life's
Woodleaf, nestled in the Sierra Nevada foothills.*

~

*"Our friends are Jesus, disguised as kids with disabilities. Whatever we do with them, and how we do it with them, is done to Jesus. Never forget that, because I know I won't."*

~

We had never taken kids in wheelchairs to camp before and really didn't know what to expect. I thought we had plenty of leaders, an almost one-to-one ratio. It turned out I should've brought 10 more!

During the four-hour trip to Woodleaf we stopped at a Burger King for dinner. As we got the kids out of the van, I saw people staring at us from inside the restaurant. What did they think we were? Aliens exiting a flying saucer? I was embarrassed, angry and uncomfortable. (Yes, I was still working on being comfortable with being uncomfortable.) How could people be so openly rude? I was getting a little taste of what happens every day to people with disabilities.

We entered the packed restaurant and maneuvered around people with our friends in wheelchairs, searching for suitable tables. People cut in front of us and ran into us. When we sat down to eat and help feed our friends, I couldn't help noticing people staring at – even talking about – us. It really started bothering me.

Soon, my friend Antwon had to use the restroom. Getting him there was like navigating an obstacle course. The entrance to the restroom was narrow and zigzagged, causing Antwon's chair to get stuck. Ugh! We couldn't get him in the door. No access. Like Jesus at the Bethlehem inn, there was no room. Accommodating a wheelchair-bound person wasn't part of the design strategy for this restroom's entrance.

In that moment I entered more deeply into Antwon's world. Obstacles. Stares. Inaccessibility.

We finally had to back Antwon out, tearing off a piece of the door jamb in the process. "Quick, let's get out of here!" I said to my fellow leader, Mike. I felt like we were going to be arrested for property damage and lectured about inconveniencing the line of annoyed people behind us trying to get into the restroom. We loaded up the vans and headed out on the last leg of the journey to Woodleaf. I was so glad to leave that stressful situation in order to get to…an even more stressful situation!

I had been to Woodleaf countless times, but never with kids in wheelchairs. The expansive camp's hills and gravel paths had never been a problem before, but all that changed as we attempted to help our friends travel in their electric wheelchairs. Every time we went up a hill their tires would spin out. We had to push the wheelchairs, each of which weighed hundreds of pounds.

The first camp event that day had groups of kids racing in a circuit around the camp. We couldn't keep up with the others, arriving at the station to join our group, just as they were finishing the activity. Then the able-bodied kids were off to the next location, leaving us in the dust. So frustrating! By the time we finished the entire circuit, our leaders were completely exhausted, but none of them complained.

That evening we entered the Club room for our first activity, but no one came over to us. We were like the plague. Once again, I felt myself embarrassed and angry. Can we possibly fit in here? It was obvious that the able-bodied kids were scared to get close to us, just like I was when I first met my friends. High school students don't automatically reach out to anyone who doesn't appear capable of making them look cool in front of their peers. Greeting, let alone hanging out with our group of kids, was social suicide. What amazed and surprised me was how my friends just took it all in stride. They weren't upset with the not-so-subtle discrimination, even though I was steaming mad.

As the evening came to an end, I couldn't wait to get to our cabins and go to sleep. I didn't have a clue about preparing the cabin and accommodations for our kids. Once inside, we discovered that our cabin was completely inaccessible, including the bathroom and shower.

We got the kids inside and began trying to get them ready for bed. We were basically clueless as to how we should do it). My 18-year-old leaders kept asking me what to do. My wise and sensitive reply was, "I don't know, ask them." Two hours later, we still did not have kids ready for bed. It was 1 a.m. Looking around me, I fell into an abyss of stress. To add to the discouragement, we were going to have to wake up before we got to sleep in order to get kids ready for breakfast! Being the seasoned, godly and completely amazing leader I am, I immediately came up with a plan, and implemented it!

I dashed out of the cabin, deserting my leaders and the kids, and ran to the lake.

For 45 minutes I angrily yelled at God. Like Moses, I ranted and raved, telling Him, "I can't do this and I knew I couldn't! You tricked me into this, God. I quit. I will stay here through the weekend, but I am serving You my resignation papers on Monday."

Yeah, I sure told God off. Then I headed back to the cabin, feeling worse than ever. To my great surprise, my awesome leaders had gotten everyone in bed (no thanks to me). I marveled, but I was too angry to let that thought deliver me out of my self-pity. A little after 2 a.m. I wearily crawled up into my top bunk, upset, steam still coming out of my ears. I finally began to doze off when I heard a voice below me calling my name.

"Nick. Nick!" It was Antwon, who had muscular dystrophy. "Nick!"

No way was I going to respond. "Come on, someone, don't you hear him? I thought. I just wanted to go to sleep.

"Nick, Nick," Antwon continued pleading. No one but me heard him.

Completely annoyed, I finally blurted out, "What?" hoping my curt tone would stop him from annoying me.

"Turn me." Antwon replied.

"Turn yourself." I said.

"I can't." he replied.

Incredulous and angry, I climbed down the ladder and came to his bunk. I grabbed the edge of his blanket and pulled hard so his body turned over. "Now, go to sleep!"

"Thanks, Nick."

As I look back on that episode today, I am amazed at God's grace towards me during one of my worst moments. If I was God, I would have struck me down with lightning. Or, perhaps more appropriately, with a wheelchair. Thankfully, God loves us even at our worst and uses us when we have nothing left. Jesus met me in that cabin and dealt with me, changing me forever.

As I climbed up the ladder to my bunk after turning Antwon, I heard Jesus. Not audibly, but in my spirit and as if He had a microphone. "Nick!" I froze. "Nick! It's **Me** you turned! It's Me you fed! It's Me you stood by when no one else would. It's me you took to the bathroom. It's Me."

Listening, I collapsed on my bunk in a state of wonder and awe. Tears streaming down my face, I asked, "How can a person's life make a 180-degree turn while climbing a five-rung ladder? Well, mine did because Jesus met me there.

He called me, not at my best, but at my worst. And, He revealed to me who my friends really were and who He really was. What a transformation in my perspective! Not only are these not kids to be pitied, but we can meet Jesus in and through them in the most powerful of ways. I sure did that night.

I awakened my leaders early and gathered them together to let them know what had happened to me the night before. I told them, "Our friends are Jesus, disguised as kids with disabilities. Whatever we do with them, and how we do it with them, is done to Jesus. Never forget that, because I know I won't."

Later that morning, after Club, we gathered our friends for cabin time in the Club room. We discussed what the speaker told us about Jesus. Antwon said, "I've never been to a place this beautiful. I looked at the trees and I prayed to God. I asked him to be my friend." Antwon was our first kid to meet Christ and, yet I had met Christ myself in a life-changing way through Antwon the night before.

That began a 20-year friendship with Antwon. He outlived his muscular dystrophy by 15 years, but died at the age of 36. In the last couple of years of his life, Antwon called me weekly and he would recall all the things we did together over the years.

"Nick, remember when you took us to the theater to see the new 'Star Trek' movie? Remember when we would have Bible study at 6 in the morning at your house? With doughnuts and chocolate! Remember when I pied you in the face? Remember when we would sing 'King Jesus is All?' That's my testimony song." Antwon always ended his phone calls by saying, "Nick, be encouraged! I am praying for you and your family!"

Conducting his funeral was one of the greatest honors of my life. The little church was packed with people Antwon had touched and changed (like me), and I got to tell everyone about a life too short, but so well lived. A life that was the aroma of Christ to all he met. Antwon's life was like a costly perfume that came in a defective bottle.

After the funeral I bought a bright red sweatshirt and in dark blue letters had this inscribed on it:

## Be Encouraged!
Antwon

When I coached my two sons' Little League team that year, I wore that sweatshirt to our team's first practice and told the kids about Antwon. I told them I was dedicating the season to him and, in honor of him, we were always going to be positive as a team and encouraging to each other. "If someone strikes out or makes an error we will still say, 'Be encouraged!'"

Other teams had players with more baseball skills than us, but we went on a 16-game winning streak after a 0-and-5 start. We made it to the championship game, but were getting pounded 15-2. In the middle of an11-run inning against us, our kids on the field started yelling to each other, "Be encouraged! Don't give up. Be encouraged!"

We rallied but ended up losing 15-14, with the tying run on first when the last out was made. Twenty years after Antwon changed my life, God used his words to inspire a group of 10-year-olds in a game they will never forget.

From my friend, Antwon, I learned that God's power is made perfect in weakness. I learned that my weaknesses and flaws, the stuff I so anxiously attempt to cover up, are embraced by God as He does His greatest work. From Antwon I learned I could choose to be encouraged - no matter what I faced - when I realized God was there with me.

Consider: What are your strengths? What are your weaknesses? How have you seen God use you in your weaknesses? May you be encouraged!

# Giving a Voice
# to the Voiceless

*By 1983 I had become great friends with the kids I met*
*in the high-school cafeteria three years before. I loved heading*
*to the campus to spend time with my friends.*

★☆ ★☆★

*One of the things we say is,*
*"Take the unhurried time to come alongside a*
*kid and listen, and then you will hear a voice."*
*For those who cannot speak for themselves,*
*we will be their voice! I think that's one*
*reason why Jesus said, repeatedly,*
*"He who has ears to hear, let him hear."*

One Monday at lunch I realized I had been having the same weekly conversations with my friends for the past three years. The trouble was I had not really heard what they were telling me. Not until the day when the Lord, graciously, gave me ears to really hear.

After three years of visits and growing relationships, when I walked into the cafeteria I was a superstar, a rock star, a Hollywood celebrity, the President of the United States, and the ambassador to Jupiter. Not really, but that's the way my friends made me feel every time I came to see them. "Nick! Nick!" they screamed with delight. "Hey gang, what's happening?" I would inquire as I gave high-fives and hugs all around.

Then I asked, "What did you all do this weekend?"

"Nothing," said Donna.

"Nothing," said Mike.

"TV," said Albert.

After years of hearing the same answers every lunchtime, I challenged them. "Hey, you guys always tell me the same thing. Come on, who got together on Friday night?" Silence. "Who went to the homecoming dance?" Blank stares. "Anyone been to *any* of the dances this year?" Nothing. I asked about every school activity there was. Not one of my friends had been to any school activity at any time. I couldn't believe what I was hearing. Or, I should say, not hearing.

The most poignant moment in the conversation that day was when I looked at my friends Lillian and Cesar, who had been boyfriend and girlfriend for two years, and asked, "What about you two? When was your last date?" Cesar replied, "We have never had a date. We have no way of going places." I was shaken.

My friends were like everyone else, with the same kinds of desires and dreams. The difference was that they not only didn't have much of a voice to express their desires, the world around them didn't hear them.

Listening to and really hearing many of my friends takes a substantial effort, because some of them have slurred speech or are nonverbal. Good listening means slowing down and paying close attention in order to catch the full meaning of their words. My friends were gracious enough to slow down and teach me how to hear, not just listen.

What I didn't realize then was that by stopping, listening and truly hearing our friends, we strengthen their voice and became part of their community. It's an unusual community of caring adults, able-bodied high-school kids, and kids of every color and ethnic background with disabilities: a community formed around the brokenness that Christ desires.

It's a brokenness we all desperately need. Even though none of us seeks brokenness, God uses it to complete our wholeness. Recognizing our brokenness is how we prepare so God's glory can enter our lives.

With a new understanding of kids with disabilities and our desire to enter into community with them, I went to my Young Life area director and told him, "I know this might sound crazy, but I think we are supposed to start a Club for my friends with disabilities."

When we started our Club I recruited every friend I had, a small army of energetic, committed people. We took our friends with disabilities everywhere: the mall, bowling, San Francisco, amusement parks, baseball games, hiking, fishing, and skiing. Why? Because we wanted our friends to have the same opportunities as their peers.

Apart from our involvement in their lives, those opportunities were not going to happen.

But there was more. We wanted to bring our friends to the feet of Jesus, who loved people with disabilities when He walked the earth. And something else happened that I didn't expect. Personal friends I had recruited as leaders fell in love with our Club kids. They actually became good friends!

These new leaders were just like me at first – uncomfortable with being uncomfortable – but they didn't give up. As they began to know kids and understand them, they developed deep friendships. With changed hearts they returned to their groups of friends, families, schools, churches and cities. They looked around and said, "Why can't we start Capernaum right here? Right now!" Without even knowing it, they had become voices and advocates for our friends.

When we went out in public the staring was still there, but some people were bold enough to approach and ask what was going on. I realized how strange it is to our world to see a group of kids in wheelchairs, cutting up with each other, doing the same things as their peers do.

But the most powerful voices for the voiceless were within my own ministry, Young Life. As we involved our friends in Clubs, camps and other activities, it slowly but powerfully began affecting the Young Life family and culture. When I spoke about our ministry, people were often shocked and shed tears. "I had no idea," they told me. "I never thought about these kids." God had made us a prophetic voice within our own organization.

Danny was a kid I really loved. His disability was severe. He was non-verbal and needed total care. One day I went to his high-school campus, accompanied by a woman who wanted to volunteer. She was a sharp, high-powered executive in a very successful business and graciously wanted to give some of her time to our kids.

After introducing her to my friends, I got lost in a conversation with Antwon. When I looked back, she was standing off to the side staring at Danny, who was being fed. She had the same look on her face that I must have had when I first entered the cafeteria years ago. Walking back to the parking lot she asked me, "Why do you do this? Is there anything inside of them?"

Because of my own experience, I understood her attitude and felt compassion. I simply said, "You know that boy you were watching? He has a name and it's Danny. He's crazy about Elvis, his favorite sport is soccer and he loves to sing."

"But he can't talk," she protested. "How do you know what he likes?"

"Because I've taken the time to get to know him, to find out how he communicates, to learn what's inside him."

She shook her head in unbelief, drove off and didn't volunteer with us. I was saddened that this competent, caring woman could not see my friends as I did. But, it wouldn't be the first time. Whenever it happens, I feel a little bit like Jesus might have felt with His disciples when He asked them, "You are not going to leave also, are you?" Those of us who love our friends get discouraged and hurt when we see them rejected by those we bring near to meet them.

We are a voice for our friends' families as well. Stereotypes, ignorance and misunderstandings persist because most people don't understand the world of our friends with disabilities. Their families must deal with broken marriages, frequent medical needs and inadequate transportation to a greater degree than most families. At

Capernaum, we have the privilege of giving respite and enrichment to the parents of our friends.

One of the things we say is, "Take the unhurried time to come alongside a kid and listen. Then, you will hear a voice. For those who cannot speak for themselves, we will be their voice! I think that's one reason why Jesus said, repeatedly, 'He who has ears to hear, let him hear.'"

I saw this acted out so powerfully at a summer camp years ago. It was an experience that showed me we are not only a voice for the voiceless, but we can give kids with disabilities opportunities to find and express their own voices.

It happened at a special seminar on self-esteem. The 70 kids attending were fairly typical of most high school students - beautiful, talented, everything going for them (at least by outward appearances).

One of my friends, Petey, came to the seminar, too. Petey has spina bifida. He rolled his chair into the middle of the room early, while the other kids sat on the floor around him. Petey stuck out like a sore thumb, in more ways than one.

The seminar got started and after about 10 minutes of lightweight comments, Petey startled all of us by shouting through his tears, "I want a job! I want to be a Young Life Capernaum leader like Nick. And, I want to get married."

The room went silent.

Then the sound of soft weeping filled the room. But the tears weren't for Petey. Petey had forced open a door of vulnerability and for the next hour, kids poured their hearts out over the pain they felt inside over appearance, self-hatred, depression, and fear.

In other words, they cried out their (internal) disabilities. When Petey expressed his longings, it triggered what able-bodied kids also feel, but hide. Petey's courage opened the door for his peers to express their unfulfilled desires, as well as the painful and broken places in their lives.

Petey had been given a time and place to use his voice, and he took advantage of the chance to speak the truth, to speak his heart. But that wasn't all. His voice gave all his good-looking, talented and seemingly self-assured peers a voice for their own hidden pain and very real disabilities.

After that week I received a letter from two beautiful able-bodied girls who were at the camp when Petey spoke out.

*"We had planned to kill ourselves right after camp. But, when we saw those smiling kids you brought up in wheelchairs all week, we knew that if they could smile with all they go through, then there had to be a God. So, we talked to God and decided to follow Him."*

Petey and his friends had given these two girls a voice for their pain, voices ready to cry out to God. As we give voice to the voiceless, Christ comes in His full glory and meets all of us. Those deep friendships can help us find our voice to speak out for our friends, and help them as they find their own voices.

Last summer I brought a team to the beautiful Hawaiian island of Kauai to put together a day camp for our newest Capernaum ministry. One of the boys who attended was 21-year-old Josh – non-verbal, very sharp, and needing full care. He had the time of his life. On the last night we held a celebration for the parents, sharing with them about their kids' amazing week. Josh had worked all that day on a speech about his week, and recorded it on his computerized voice box. We listened, amazed:

*"My name is Josh. I am 21. I have felt depressed all my life because of the burden I am to my parents. But this week I found out how much God loves me. I found hope. I know God has a future for me and I am going to trust Him for it."*

He then had a song played that captured the events and feelings of his week. As the song played, his parents came up in tears and embraced their son. Then, an even more incredible thing happened: All 17 of the campers came up and surrounded Josh, embracing him, stroking his hair, arms, and back. Kids were responding to Josh because he had voiced so eloquently what they could not. He was their champion, their voice in a world that refused to take time to listen.

This is one of the great needs Capernaum fulfills. We are a group of people who hear voices. We hear God's voice saying, "Go to the voiceless; the kids with unheard voices who long for friendship, adventure, understanding, belonging, and purpose." After hearing them, we join our voices with theirs, declaring the incredible value of their personhood over their disabilities.

> **Consider:** Is there something inside you that you've never been able to voice? What has been the result? Would you be willing to come alongside a young person with a disability and listen for their voice? If so, you just might find your own.

( **5** )

# A Season of Firsts

*They say there's a first time for everything, and a*
*ministry to kids with disabilities certainly*
*validates that saying.*

~

*These young leaders served in a way best
described by Joni Eareckson Tada:
"Special-needs ministry is Christianity
with its sleeves rolled up."*

~

The firsts for kids with disabilities and for those who serve them are many. It's a choice to walk in faith, courage, creativity and flexibility for the first time ever. It's a choice to overcome the obstacles and pave an accessible, welcoming road for kids so they can get to destinations of adventure and belonging. It's a choice to help kids get to Christ.

Capernaum, like most first-time ventures, began with small steps. I love Zechariah 4:10 because it very well describes the launch of this ministry to kids with disabilities: "*Do not despise small beginnings.*"

In a world that worships at the altar of size, numbers and the spectacular, this ministry takes place in the world of the small and unimpressive, the insignificant, the powerless, and the unattractive. It is contrary to the world most of us know, foreign to much of the church and odd to the better-known and professional ministries. Most would probably call a ministry like Capernaum insignificant, at best, and perhaps even a failure and waste of time, money, and other resources. But, thankfully, God has a different view (see 1 Corinthians 1:26-29) and the victories our kids have achieved show we're on the right track.

"Come on, Michelle! You can do it!!"

I was the cheerleader for one of our Club kids on our first backpacking, mountain-climbing and rappelling trip for kids in wheelchairs. Michelle has cerebral palsy and she was strapped onto the back of an amazing guide named Starr. She was surrounded with other guides as Starr took her instructions from Michelle as to where to place her hands and feet as they climbed the mountain.

We had heard about Summit Adventure, an organization committed to the idea that anyone can go backpacking – including kids with disabilities – and called that part of their program the "Go-For-It Week."

As Michelle and Starr slowly made their ascent, Michelle screamed out in delight, "This is my first time climbing a mountain on someone's back!" As it turned out, it was only one of many firsts for Michelle that week.

"This is my first backpacking trip, my first time sleeping outside under the stars and the very first time I ever saw a shooting star!" But No. 1 on her list of firsts was, "This is my first time peeing in a bucket!" We exploded with laughter around the campfire that night, as Michelle giggled nonstop. Michelle and her friends not only have ushered in many first-time experiences, they've also introduced our leaders and myself to countless memorable moments.

Because there are so few people and organizations engaged in ministry with kids who have disabilities, activities are often firsts for everyone – kids, Capernaum staff and volunteers, and parents. When we started, no church in our city was doing anything with kids with disabilities. Nor was my own organization, Young Life. This was new territory. We decided we wanted kids with disabilities to experience everything their able-bodied peers experienced. As a result, we've had a parade of glorious (and terrifying) firsts.

On March 10, 1986, six years after I had met Steve, my first friend with a disability, we held our first Club. It took us 18 months to get everything in place, mainly because we had no road map or idea of what we were doing. In fact, we failed to launch that first Club for three weeks in a row! We were almost ready to give up, but decided to try one more time. I'm so glad we didn't quit, because that brand-new, never-done-it-before Club gave me one of the greatest days of my life.

Over the years, the kids themselves were the pioneers. We invited and coaxed them, but unless they had trusted us, there would have been no Capernaum ministry. When I think of all the things we did together, like mountain climbing and skiing, two words come to mind: faith and courage!

Back to our first Club meeting. That morning, as I steered our leased, lift-equipped van into the Blackford High School driveway, five kids in wheelchairs appeared. They screamed and pumped their arms in the air as if they had just won the lottery. "What are they so excited about?" I wondered. "They haven't even been to Club yet."

But I was missing the point of what that first Club represented to my new friends. Their world was all about boredom, no activities and no opportunities to make new friends. They were hungry for something outside of their school and homes, something they could call their own.

When we headed off to Club it was with five kids in wheelchairs, four able-bodied high school kids and four leaders. What an incredible hour! They devoured the whole experience like someone who hadn't eaten for a week. It wasn't what I was used to with able-bodied kids. The hour wasn't smooth or flowing, so compared to a typical Young Life Club it seemed like a failure. But the kids went ballistic over it! I had never seen such excitement in a Club.

In a world with few opportunities, Capernaum offered dozens of possibilities, each of which they joyfully received. *"Blessed are the poor in spirit for theirs is the kingdom of heaven."* (Matt. 5:3) Their lives weren't overcrowded with busyness and many of the other idols in our culture. They had space for God and all God wanted to give them through their new Capernaum friends.

Maybe you're wondering who supports an endeavor like Capernaum. Who and why have hundreds become closely involved with the kids we serve? The answers may surprise you.

Although some of our supporters had no interest in the Christian message at the core of the ministry, they cared a great deal about the kids. There are a lot of people willing to financially support a ministry like this because of the satisfaction they find by encouraging these precious young people. For some donors it is because they have a friend or family member with a disability. Others were grabbed by the extent to which our volunteers serve the disabled community.

Our first donors were the Kerley family. Ken and Alice Kerley's son had died tragically years before, and they wanted to get involved financially as a way of honoring their son's memory. Being part of Capernaum was healing for them.

My first leadership team was comprised mainly of my Club kids who had recently graduated from high school. I asked them to be part of this new thing and they adventurously said "Yes!" to something uniquely challenging and completely unfamiliar. They jumped into their roles and served, even when some other Young Life leaders told them Capernaum wasn't part of the "real" Young Life.

These young leaders served in a way best described by Joni Eareckson Tada: "Special-needs ministry is Christianity with its sleeves rolled up." I agree. This opportunity requires giving all of oneself to another, caring for them physically, spiritually, emotionally, and mentally.

Our team's prayer was that Capernaum would spread around the world in our lifetimes, reaching every kid with a disability in every country around the globe. Two years later we celebrated the first answer to that prayer. The second Capernaum ministry began in Colorado Springs, and the ministry continues to grow around the world.

One of my first leaders was Mike Morrison. After his senior year, I took him to camp and he began his relationship with Jesus. Mike didn't know what he really wanted to do after high school, and thought about joining the armed forces. I had another idea. "Mike, why don't you stay in San Jose? I will be available to you for the coming year, helping you grow in your relationship with Christ while you help me in this new ministry I am forming, called Capernaum."

Mike agreed and volunteered with us for the next 26 years! I discovered that Mike was one of the greatest servants I've ever known. All I did was point him toward kids and encourage him. He and God did the rest.

One of our first outings was to Marriott's Great America with six of our Club kids. In six hours we were able to board a grand total of three rides; I learned that it takes more people to help - for a longer period of time doing much less than usual - when it comes to our friends with disabilities.

With each new activity and location we attempted, there was something new to learn. Part of my own education process was learning to set aside my usual mode of seeing kids only as able-bodied. I had a lot to learn and my friends with disabilities were my first teachers. There are huge differences between being with kids in a Club setting and moving around with those same kids in public places. The challenges include inaccessible facilities and unpredictable health issues that require constant flexibility.

At the end of the day it seemed like we had done so few of the activities at Great America, I thought it was a colossal failure and that the kids would never want to do anything with us again. I was corrected on the van ride home when they all said it was the greatest day of their lives. Antwon, from the back of the van, yelled out, "When are we going again?"

One day at the high school campus, the bell rang ending the lunch period just as one of my friends, Bob, called out, "Nick, take me to the bathroom. I need help." I looked around in panic to find someone else to take him. Soon, Bob was yelling, "Nick, now!" "But, Bob, I don't know what to do. I've never taken anyone to the bathroom." Bob calmly and firmly shot back, "Nick, I'll tell you what to do. Just take me."

So off we went. It was the first of many times I would attend to kids' physical needs. It was an intimidating lesson in one of the most sacred tasks of our ministry; learning to care for another's body.

Now, if you recoil at that and think you could never take on a task like I did with Bob, I understand. Let me remind you, however, that I had never done any of this before in my life. But, I did it because they were my friends. And friends help friends. We are not professionals in the field of disability. We are friends who enter kids' worlds to serve and learn.

In a ministry to kids with disabilities, we've come to expect a certain amount of disappointment. Sometimes a volunteer won't follow through when their help is badly needed. Sometimes parents are so protective of their kids that they won't let them come to Club or participate in activities with their friends. But we've discovered that disappointment becomes an opportunity for challenge and change, even for victory. Here's what I mean.

My first really big disappointment made me realize that as we enter our friends' world we identify with – even take on – their sufferings. Their disappointments become our disappointments, their hurts begin to make us hurt, too. In this way we literally share in the sufferings of Christ, because our friends with disabilities are Jesus disguised as someone with a disability.

Once I took Antwon and about 40 able-bodied kids roller skating. This is perfect, I thought to myself. Antwon was already on wheels and he could roll with the other kids around the rink. After about one lap around the rink the arena operator, using his best I'm-the-boss voice, announced over the PA, "Will the wheelchair immediately leave the rink? You cannot be on the skating rink."

I could not believe what I was hearing and was crushed as I watched Antwon dejectedly leave the rink. It was horrible for him – a complete and extremely public rejection. At that moment I had another first-time experience: being a voice and an advocate for Antwon (and learning to channel my anger constructively!).

I approached the skating-rink announcer and asked, "Do you realize what you just did?" He claimed he had to follow the company's liability policy (which made me laugh - Antwon was safer than anyone on the rink). I told him the problem wasn't the rink's policy, but how it was communicated. The public humiliation had deeply embarrassed a kid in front of 40 other kids. I suggested how the announcer could have done it differently, in a discreet way that would not have embarrassed Antwon. There wasn't much of a response, but at least Antwon heard me sticking up for him, while sharing in his disappointment.

At the end of our first year of Club I experienced a part of our friends' experience that is truly tragic: The first of the 25 kids in our ministry who have died over the past 26 years was taken from us. In May of our first year Steve, a 20-year-old with muscular dystrophy, died. He had Duchene's muscular dystrophy, a killer that strikes kids between 14 and 21 years old suddenly and terribly. Steve loved Club and asked Christ into his life two weeks before he died. He was the first of a long line of kids we loved so much, kids who went to be with the Lord.

That first death ushered me into a world of surgeries, hospital stays and funerals. Many kids with disabilities die without their friends nearby because those closest to them don't have transportation to visit the hospital or attend the funeral. Too many kids experience decline and death way too early in their lives. These kids experience loss with open, excruciating grief. They feel the loss of relationships to a greater degree than most others, since their relationships are the biggest thing in their lives.

All these firsts with my friends have made me realize the truth of Jesus' upside-down statement, "The first shall be last and the last shall be first." At Capernaum, our first order of business is the kids our culture considers the least and the last.

*Brothers and sisters, look at what you were when God called you. Not many of you were wise in the way the world judges wisdom. Not many of you had great influence. Not many of you come from important families. But God chose the foolish things of the world to shame the strong. He chose what the world thinks is unimportant and what the world looks down on and thinks is nothing in order to destroy what the world thinks is important. God did this so no one can brag in His presence. I Cor. 1:26-29.*

**Consider:** With the heart for kids with disabilities God has given you, take the next step. How could you meet a kid with a disability? Take the brave step of a first conversation.

# 6

# Hidden in Plain Sight

*We were at Pizza Hut eating, laughing
and enjoying each other's company;
10 kids and a group of leaders.*

~

*...at that moment, John was literally hidden in plain sight, visibly invisible. I was beginning to understand how unseen my friends were - even when they were right out in the open.*

~

My slice of pizza was interrupted by one of my wonderful friends named John. He needed the restroom and I agreed to go with him and help. John maneuvered his very large wheelchair through the packed restaurant, toward the restroom. After about 10 minutes of waiting in line we finally made it to the front.

As the restroom door opened and we began to move toward the door, a man behind us darted around us. Before he entered I shouted, "Hey! We were next!" He stopped, looked back at John with surprise and exclaimed, "Oh, I'm sorry. I didn't see him."

Didn't see him? John is a big kid and occupies an even bigger wheelchair. But at that moment, John was literally hidden in plain sight, visibly invisible. I was beginning to understand how unseen my friends were - even when they were right out in the open.

Restaurants aren't the only places where this kind of selective blindness occurs. Once, I had a booth set up at a ministry fair. Very few people showed any interest, which is normal for this type of ministry. One well-dressed gentleman walked up to our booth and grabbed one of our brochures. As he browsed it he said, "Disability ministry. There can't be much of a market for that." With that frosty declaration he walked away, intent on visiting the more appealing ministries nearby.

Despite being troubled by the concept of combining market and ministry to produce a viable commodity, I did not have a chance to show this man how big the disability "market" really is. Here are some of the raw facts about a global community that's hidden in plain sight:

- Worldwide, there are more than 600 million people with disabilities.
- If that group was a nation it would be the world's third-largest and would lead the world in both homelessness and poverty.

- More than 50 million Americans have a disability, including 15 percent of all teens. (It's revealing and an indictment, frankly, that we do not see this percentage represented in our churches' youth groups. Only 10 percent of all churches are engaged in or planning a ministry to people with disabilities. Ministries to teens with disabilities are almost nonexistent in American churches.)
- 18 million people in the world need wheelchairs but don't have them.

Yes, the numbers are huge and the needs are overwhelming. What's worse, the presence of people with disabilities' in the church is minimal. "Hey, if there are so many people with disabilities," people ask, "then where are they? I haven't seen any in a long time." The answer to the "Where are they" question is found in the opening story of this chapter. Kids like John and others with disabilities can be right in front of us - in plain sight – and, yet, be hidden.

The problem is us and our vision. We have a disability of our own: our inability to see things as they truly are. We look without really seeing.

Part of the issue is that we're taught it is impolite to stare at anyone, especially in public. So, when we encounter someone with a disability, we try not to stare. So far, so good. But by not staring we end up not seeing accurately. God wants to heal the biased, even prejudiced blindness that causes us to overlook our friends with disabilities.

I have firsthand experience with this particular visual affliction because until that visit to campus in the fall of 1980, I never noticed kids with disabilities. Meeting my friends in that cafeteria opened my eyes to see what had been hidden in plain sight. All of a sudden it seemed like kids with disabilities were everywhere! It's similar to when you buy a yellow car and you start seeing them everywhere. The number of yellow autos hasn't changed, but your ability to notice them has! Your eyes are opened.

My friend Kent opened one of our fundraising banquets by saying, "I grew up being told not to stare at people with disabilities. That's OK, but the problem then becomes one of not seeing them at all! We need new eyes, so we can stare, but in a brand-new way."

Kent's words helped transform my own eyesight. When I saw people in wheelchairs on the sidewalk while I was driving, I stared. But I looked for a new reason. Not to gawk at an alien or gaze with pity. Instead, I was looking to see if it was one of my Club kids or someone else who might be interested in Capernaum Club.

We need new eyes from Jesus to see the invisible people in our culture. But there's more. When our eyes are opened to those hidden to us, we see something else. We begin to see ourselves. Why have I been so blind? Why didn't I notice? What's going on with me? I am part of a culture that includes millions of people with disabilities, but we're blind to them and refuse to acknowledge them, let alone welcome them.

Another reason we don't see them is that our media and cultural focus is on those who are bright, beautiful, and productive. With our attention focused on the so-called best and brightest, we're unaware of people with disabilities. In our churches, students in our youth groups can often be blindly inhospitable to kids with disabilities.

The truth is, my friends are bright, beautiful and productive, but in ways that are largely unknown in our culture. Here's what God's restoration work on my eyes has accomplished:

- I see intelligence and caring when kids are aware that their friend, seated behind them in a van, is having a silent seizure.

They can't turn around to see and support her because they
are strapped into their wheelchairs, but they know she is
having one.

- I see the bright emotional, social and relational competence
  these special kids bring to the lives of others.
- I see beautiful when I watch the wide-eyed smiles on the
  faces of kids as they dance in self-effacing joy, filling the air
  around them with beauty.
- I see productivity when I see one kid feeding another kid
  who can't feed himself and when ambulatory kids push
  their friends who are confined to wheelchairs. This is God's
  idea of productivity - helping others.

There are countless other places where kids with disabilities
are hidden in plain sight. There are hundreds of thousands of kids in
group homes, children's hospitals, rehab clinics and special-education
schools most people don't even know exist. Three years ago we began a
ministry in a small residential facility that had a hospital and a school.

The 50 kids, from infants to 22-year-olds, have severe disabilities,
including some in non-responsive states. The kids in these facilities
have parents who are unable to care for their children. Or, the parents
did not want them and abandoned them. Some kids have never seen
their parents.

The people in these kinds of places rarely receive visitors. The
isolation, boredom and loneliness they experience are debilitating.
(During Capernaum's first year, I heard about kids in situations like
this and prayed we would have a presence with them. Twenty-three
years later, God answered that prayer.)

This facility, filled with kids who have little contact with the
outside world, is located in a residential area. Yes, hidden in plain
sight. Hidden among the hidden are the kids in nonresponsive states,

precious ones to whom we can read or play music. Why? Because, as one of the therapists said, "There's a sacred soul inside and if it were me I would want touch, reading, and music, whatever I could possibly receive from someone else."

Sometimes a very well-known person enters the world of disability unexpectedly; the highly visible becomes extremely invisible. A beautiful young woman named Carol was a star athlete at her high school, but her life changed forever after a tragic car accident. She ended up at the acute-care hospital, facing a long rehabilitation challenge. Her life slowly moved from attention to anonymity. Hidden in plain sight.

A few years back I took a small team to the Dominican Republic to begin Capernaum there. With the local Young Life director we went to homes where she suspected there were kids with disabilities. We did our best to obey the command of Luke 14 and the parable of the Great Banquet. Jesus sent us, His servants, to find where "the lame, the crippled, the blind, and the poor" were. We found 10 kids, literally hidden away in their homes.

Five days later we held the first Capernaum Club, with a team of 14 Dominican leaders, 50 relatives and friends, and the 10 kids who had never left their homes! The Club lasted four hours. No one wanted to go home. Like the paralytic Jesus healed (see Mark 2:1-12), these kids were brought out of hiding into public view. They were restored to community.

In 1990 one of my dearest Capernaum friends, Mike, died of complications from muscular dystrophy. A memorial was held for Mike on campus during a school day, on the lawn in the quad. All Mike's friends from the special-education class they attended together were gathered in a circle of wheelchairs. We shared memories of Mike until the bell rang, signaling the end of the school day.

As the usual stampede out of the classrooms began, a constant stream of kids walked through Mike's memorial circle. What seemed completely obvious to us was completely un-obvious to many of the 1800 kids leaving school that day.

As kids paraded through I stopped one and asked, "Hey, do you see what's going on here?" The student looked at our group and said, "No. What is this? "It is a memorial service for our friend who just died", I replied. "Oh, wow!" he said slowly. "Sorry, I was in a hurry and didn't see you guys." Almost as tragic as his death was the fact that to many of his classmates, Mike was as invisible in death as he'd been in life.

Over the years, God has used a variety of Young Life Capernaum people and events to give us all new eyes. At our fund-raising banquet, kids got to share their stories with hundreds of people. The tears flowed as the listeners' eyes were opened to see kids who had suddenly became very visible and human. During summer camp, 10 Capernaum kids mixed with 300 able-bodied kids. Our friends' courage to do everything at camp opened the eyes of their peers. When we took 20 kids in wheelchairs to the mall for ice cream, our laughter was loud...and contagious. People came up to us, asking "What is this?" And I got to tell them about my friends.

If we hear and comprehend the full meaning of Jesus' mandate to reach "the least of these," we have a choice whether we'll say "Yes." If our response is positive we'll find joy and purpose in finding kids and building deep friendships with them. This is costly. It means consistent, patient, unhurried time with kids. It means keeping your word to the kids and families who are used to empty talk and broken promises.

Capernaum wants to help others receive new eyesight from God, so they can see these precious-but-invisible kids. That's when the miracles happen. That's when people begin to discover the kids they had overlooked, the kids they had not seen or gotten to know. When they do, they find out what the disciples did when they encountered a blind man on the side of the road.

The disciples concluded (incorrectly) that the cause of the man's blindness was sin; they just didn't know if the sin was his or his parents'. Jesus' reply obliterates their assumption. Not only did the man's disability have nothing to do with his or his parents' sin, Jesus said he was born that way to show the glory of God. (John 9:3) God's glory may seem hidden, but for those with eyes to see, it is on public display through kids with disabilities.

How about you? Do you see God's glory revealed in kids with disabilities?

**Consider:** Do some research and find out where kids with disabilities are in your community.

## 7

# The Killer App

*"One hundred years from now our society will
look back in shame on how we treated people with disabilities.
The experience will be the same as the way we looked back at the
slavery our country allowed in the earlier years of its history."*

~

*People with disabilities have been in an exodus
from their own slavery and dark ages.
The entire world is just now waking up
to the shameful ways we have
treated people with disabilities.*

~

In 1990 the small group of us doing Capernaum traveled to Germany on a disabilities study trip. Young Life was partnering with a group of German Christians who were actively ministering with persons with disabilities and we were eager to learn from them. It was inspiring to see the amazing things our German brothers and sisters were doing to care for people with disabilities in their nation.

We visited a small, beautiful church that was involved in special-needs ministry. As I sat in the front pew, the pastor pointed to the altar. A large book lay at its center, with a much-smaller one on the right. Not surprisingly, the larger and more prominently placed book was the Bible. The pastor then pointed to the smaller book and said, "This book contains the names of people with disabilities in this parish who Hitler executed in the gas chambers of a concentration camp." We sat in stunned silence.

When I began Capernaum, I wanted all the help I could get. One friend, Leslie, worked as an advocate for people with disabilities with the Los Angeles city council. Her response to my request for advice was unexpected, to say the least. "I will not give you any advice, Nick. I will only tell you that 100 years from now our society will look back in shame on how we treated people with disabilities. The experience will be the same as the way we looked back at the slavery our country allowed in the earlier years of its history."

I couldn't believe she was serious. That is, until I dug a little deeper. It wasn't until the mid-'70s that people with disabilities were guaranteed architectural and educational access in our country. And it wasn't until 1990 that civil rights were guaranteed to persons with disabilities through the landmark Americans with Disabilities Act (ADA).

Let that sink in. It's been only 38 years since educational and architectural access was granted for people with disabilities. Just 23 years since a comprehensive package of civil rights was finally secured.

The view that people with disabilities are tragedies paves the way for actions that echo Hitler's own strategies. Ninety percent of Down-syndrome-diagnosed babies are aborted. That's right, only one out of every 10 is allowed to live! Why? Because they are viewed as mistakes, projects that would require too much of their parents, their communities, and society.

However, if there ever was a group of kids where the opposite is true, it is kids with Down syndrome. Just about any of the parents of these kids will tell you about the sorrow of an unexpected diagnosis and about the need for adjustments in their lives. They will also tell you about their angels of joy from heaven! And, how their family would be incomplete without that special person the world calls "a tragedy."

But that attitude is not widely shared. France, for example, wants to pass a law that would eliminate all Down-syndrome-diagnosed fetuses. It's nothing less than a legislated holocaust, yet few people know about the law. Even if it is approved, how many would call the result a holocaust?

While kids with disabilities are viewed as calamities by many, others consider them cursed – evidence of God's punishment for some sin or wrongdoing. What we encountered in the Dominican Republic (where we saw parents hiding their kids with disabilities indoors so no one would find out about them.) is not an isolated circumstance. This fear-based attitude can produce even greater losses. Babies with disabilities are sometimes simply abandoned and left to die.

When I started the Capernaum middle-school Club in 1990, I met a beautiful 10-year-old girl from Iran with an amazing story.

Dokie was born with a very rare disability that left her with no use of her arms or legs. Shortly after her birth the doctor told her mother and aunt, "Leave. I will take care of this." (Frightening to think about what he intended to do, isn't it?) But Dokie's aunt objected, saying, "No. I will take her and raise her as my own."

They came to America when Dokie was 8 and she flourished. Yes, her condition meant she would always need complete physical care, but she is brilliant in every way. She taught herself English by watching "The Flintstones" cartoon show on TV. By the time she began attending our Club two years later, she spoke perfect English. During the Club talks, Dokie quietly listened, every so often asking a question that was insightful and mature beyond her years.

Dokie grew up and graduated from high school. Then, using a mouth device to type all her papers, she graduated with honors from Santa Clara University. She went on to complete graduate school, and is now a professional therapist. Dokie is a gift to our world who, had it been left up to a doctor who saw her only as a tragedy and a curse, none of us would have ever known. Dokie you rock!

Then there's my friend Ruben Alvarez, with cerebral palsy. I met him when he was in his special-education school during high school, even before I started Capernaum. By age 12 he still couldn't read. No one believed he could learn anything. No one, except for one teacher. Kathy took Ruben under her wing and within a year, Ruben was reading.

Ruben also had a tremendous gift of verbal communication along with a delightful personality. He became a speech and debate champion in high school. He volunteered with us for eight years and was on staff. He married an able-bodied, former Club kid and they have three beautiful daughters. Today, Ruben is an active and effective advocate for people with disabilities. Why? Because someone looked past Ruben's disability and saw his potential.

Capernaum not only serves our friends with the good news of the Gospel and opportunities to create an active social life, we see our friends' potential to give, not just receive. My first (and quite vivid!) encounter with this reality happened with one of our first Club kids.

Lori has cerebral palsy, is in a wheelchair and requires complete care. Her speech is slurred, but Lori is very social and communicative. She persists in getting her message across until we get it.

After high school, Lori got a job at a workshop for people with disabilities. She was really excited and wanted me to see her first paycheck. It was for two weeks of work and amounted to $.26. I thought this had to be a mistake, so I called Lori's mom, Pat. "Pat, I saw Lori's paycheck. Twenty-six cents for two weeks' work? "Yes," she said, "it cost more to mail the check than what it's worth."

Pat explained that Lori's job was with a nonprofit organization that contracts out with major companies for menial work, such as folding boxes. The good news is that there is a program at all; the bad news is the poor pay and lack of dignity.

This bothered me. A lot. A year or so later, I was hanging out with Adan and our friend, Robert. During our conversation, Robert suddenly blurted out, "Man, I wish I could have a job." Remembering Lori's meager paycheck and wanting to help, I exclaimed, "I'll give you a job! Both of you!!" As I sometimes do when I'm passionate about trying to correct a dismal situation, I had spoken before jobs actually existed for Robert and Adan. My heart was so disturbed by the lack of opportunity for my friends I burned inside to do something to be an encouragement to them even though I didn't have the necessary plans in place.

I told these young men to list their best qualities and what they liked to do; their lists would help me find jobs that fit them well. They were pumped! I spent the next few days thinking, OK, Nick, where are you going to find work for these guys? You promised them jobs.

On that Friday afternoon I turned the van into the campus driveway and found Adan in a suit, slicked-back hair and looking better than Johnny Depp (and just as cool!). Because Robert had very limited resources and was from a much poorer background than Adan, his appearance really grabbed my heart. He had chosen his cleanest and best blue sweats, with the nicest shirt he could find. We headed to the Capernaum office to begin the job interviews.

Now, I knew I was going to give each of them a job, but I wanted them to go through the experience of interviewing; neither of them had ever done one. Halfway through the interview I realized how desperately they wanted the jobs! Near the end Robert anxiously asked, "Do we get the jobs?" A tear slid down my cheek as I quietly said, "Yes." I was overwhelmed as they revealed their simple and very human desire to be useful, to be wanted. In that moment I felt I was in the presence of God, the One who placed these desires in every one of us.

I told them I would give them dignified work for dignified pay. They came in two afternoons a week and completed tasks, like calling donors to thank them and tell them what was going on in our ministry. Before they began working, however, I explained why their jobs were so significant. Starting at minimum wage, they jumped into their new positions with joyful abandon and I watched as their self-esteem shot straight up.

A year later Capernaum formally began its jobs program, with $75,000 raised through my friend, Valerie. We called it the Friendship Club: Dignified Work for Dignified Pay. The program, led by my friend Donna, was a smashing success. We began and operated on the core belief that every kid with a disability is created in the image of God, with his or her own dreams, hopes, and talents to give to this world.

While interviewing each kid, we discovered their talents and dreams; previously hidden treasures that no one knew existed or bothered to talk with to them about. We were thrilled as we learned of desires and talents for gardening, painting, writing, and more. We created job titles based on their skills and passions, and then partnered them with a mentor who helped develop their talents. Our first hire after Adan and Robert was Lori! Her potential was limited, but you know what? So is mine. And so is yours.

Lori excelled socially. She never missed a birthday, anniversary or holiday without calling my family or sending a card, so we made her our Social Birthday Greeting Director. She designed greeting cards and sent them out to everyone with a birthday who was connected with our ministry. Her mentor? None other than Dokie, who had begun volunteering with us.

As we gained new eyes for our friends we increasingly saw the potential within the person - in spite of disability. We believed they were more than receivers; they could be – and wanted to be – givers. That frame of reference moves them from being marginalized to being realized. They begin to realize what they bring to the table - gifts like unrestrained joy, innocence, simplicity, unconditional love, and raw honesty. We all become more real in their presence.

A ministry like this is a decision to look past disability. A decision to see the person and discover who they are. A decision to become an advocate to our culture on their behalf so they can take their place in the community as fruitful people giving and receiving. And, yes, I'm aware that this is a fight in some places, a struggle to affirm the image of God in any person who has ever taken a breath.

**Consider:** As you begin a friendship with a kid with a disability, seek to discover some of the hidden dreams and talents that your friend possesses.

## 8

# You Can't do *That*!

*"You're stupid! This will never happen!"*
*These words were addressed to me by a gentleman at one of*
*our first meetings about starting Capernaum.*

~

*Instead of "We can't do that,"*
*we started asking, "How could we do that?"*
*and "What would it take to do that?"*

~

"You're stupid! This will never happen!"

These words were addressed to me by a gentleman at one of our first meetings about starting Capernaum. Another person believed Young Life could never be successful with kids with disabilities. Before we even started we were hit with something kids with disabilities hear constantly:

"You can't do that."

Young Life staff people told us Capernaum wasn't really Young Life. Leaders at a church explained that we couldn't use their room for kids with disabilities due to "liability reasons." We heard, "You can't take these kids backpacking," and "They won't understand the Club talk because they are delayed."

"You can't. You can't. You can't." That was the message we heard, over and over. But you know what? By God's grace that "You can't" became "You can!" Kids with disabilities are constantly facing obstacles and barriers, both the physical and attitudinal kinds. So, it's not surprising that a ministry with these friends would also encounter a myriad of obstacles like I did during that first meeting.

One of the first places we encountered the "You can't do that" attitude was in our own organization. This ministry was new, different and, for many, threatening. Some Young Life staff concluded that since Capernaum was not really Young Life (as they perceived it, anyway), we should not even think about beginning this type of ministry.

Sometimes the resistance came from local churches. When we needed a large-enough place for our Club meetings, we asked a church for permission to use one of its rooms. The leaders refused, claiming that liability and insurance issues prevented them from agreeing to our request. Their choice was based on the potential – not proven, not researched, not experienced first-hand – risk to the church.

Another obstacle for our kids was their own parents. Eighty percent of families who have kids with disabilities are single-parent families. Why? It's usually because marriages break under the immense strain that occurs when a child has a disability and because of the tremendous increase in needs that must be met. These moms and dads have faced and fought against overwhelming obstacles on behalf of their children. They are constantly being told, "No!" and "We're sorry, your child can't participate." Plus, they suffer the deep pain of watching their kids be misunderstood, rejected, and mistreated.

Then, there is the 24/7 care they must provide for their child, usually from birth into adulthood, with no end in sight. Despite these parents' challenging experiences, most have a deep and heroic love for their children. The parents of children with disabilities have my greatest respect and commitment.

Understandably, parents of kids with disabilities are especially protective. But sometimes, that well-intentioned protection inadvertently prevents their kids from experiencing the friendship, adventure and belonging which the parents want so much for their children.

Over the years we have had to earn the trust of the parents. It can be months, even years, before we are allowed to take a child out of the home. Parents have often told me, "You can't do that activity with my child. She would never be able to do that." It's so amazing to see how wonderfully surprised parents are when they find out what their son or daughter can do! "I never thought they could do that!" we've heard more than once.

When it seemed like Young Life couldn't (or wouldn't) accept this ministry I got discouraged, thinking, I can't make this grow because there are so many needs concentrated in just a few kids. Many times I felt I just couldn't go on. "It's too much. It's too hard." I'm not immune to a defeatist attitude at times. Operating from weakness, I can easily see a challenge and declare, "We can't do that!" What this really means is that I've decided I can't.

In time, however, we learned to retrain our own attitudes and voices as we became more and more involved with kids. Instead of "We can't do that," we started asking, "How could we do that?" and "What would it take to do that?"

We have chosen to make Capernaum the No. 1 place for kids with disabilities, where the first word they hear is "Yes! Yes, we can," rather than "Sorry, no, we can't." It's all in what we believe. That belief has enabled us to take kids on countless trips and adventures that seem crazy or even impossible at first glance. And the believing is not just for Capernaum staff and volunteers! Individuals, youth groups and entire churches can adopt this attitude, and flourish with kids.

Sometimes our friends with disabilities will say, "I can't do that." One of my friends, George, once told me, "I want to be a pastor, but I can't because I have a disability." Another kid tearfully said, "I can't be like other kids because I have a disability."

One of my friends, Robert, came to camp with me on his first-ever outing away from home. Despite his street smarts and familiarity with the gang and drug scene in his neighborhood, his world was very limited. He had very few experiences beyond his environment and routines.

When it came time for horseback riding, Robert and I started fighting with each other. "No, no, no, Nick. I don't want to do it," he yelled at me. It wasn't the horses that scared him; it was the thought of being lifted out of his wheelchair, high up in the air, and down into the saddle. Our little war went on for about 30 minutes as I tried to navigate the difficult and fine line between that of encouraging a kid to try something new and forcing him against his will.

Finally, Robert agreed to let the six of us (Robert was quite large) lift him from his wheelchair to the horse. After the horse took two steps, Robert said, "Get me down. Now!" And we did. What was wonderful is that despite all his fears, Robert ended up feeling excited and proud of his accomplishment. He said, "Nick, I want to try again next year, and ride longer!" Like me, Robert graduated from "I can't" to "I can."

One of the greatest and most-tragic obstacles in this ministry is the belief held by many that kids with intellectual disabilities can't comprehend the Gospel message. The doubters say, "How can they get it?" with the "it" being the good news of Jesus Christ and the new life He offers to all of us.

Let's assume for the moment that they don't get it, that they can't receive the Gospel message. Does that mean we shouldn't pursue ministry with them? Or, that Jesus died for everyone except those who cannot intellectually grasp the life-changing truth?

OK, now ask yourself, "Do I believe it's up to me alone to find and receive the Gospel?" Does your answer to that question line up with Scripture? God's Word is crystal-clear on this issue: Only the Holy Spirit brings about conversion, through His gifts of revelation, understanding, and faith. So, if that's how it works for you and me, how is it really any different for someone with an intellectual disability? Or, for that matter, with any kind of disability?

May I ask another question? Do we really believe the Holy Spirit is stymied by an intellectual disability? As my dear friend Lydia says, "Their minds might be delayed but their spirits are not." Lydia is so right. The Holy Spirit communicates to the spirit within each of us. Reaching the spirit, heart and soul of a kid with a disability presents absolutely no problem. God the Holy Spirit doesn't see one of these kids and say, "Uh, oh. I can't reach this one."

After years of seeing my friends confronted with the good news of Jesus Christ, I know that they do get it. They may get it differently than others, but I believe they get the Gospel more than most people and do so in a deep, simple, and beautiful ways.

My friend, Matt, rode home with me every week after our Club in one of our Capernaum vans. Each week on the way home he said, "Nick, I like Capernaum. I like you, Nick. I like God." That was his conviction and his heart. Was that also his conversion? I think so. What about you? What makes you agree or disagree?

This past year at Young Life's all-staff conference, a young man with Down syndrome spoke to a crowd of 4,000 about his life. He had a huge desire to give a Club talk that evening, so a big group of our Capernaum staff sat on the floor in front of him; we were his Club!

Then he spoke to us:

"Jesus was born for us.
"Jesus died for us.
"He rose on the third day.
"Jesus wants to live in our hearts."

There was a reverent silence and then we and all the other 4,000 rose in a rousing, shouting, standing ovation. It was a holy moment, achieved through a wonderful young man who avoided all the ways we make the Gospel so complicated. He lavished us in the life-changing truth of the Gospel.

Capernaum is a John-the-Baptist ministry. We work to clear the road for Jesus. We want to remove obstacles and to obliterate all the you-can't, I-can't, and they-can't statements, so the truth and power and freedom and joy of Jesus can be experienced by any and all.

Interested in being part of something incredible? Don't let anyone talk you out of investing in the kids this ministry serves, this community that says and lives, "*We can do all things through Christ who strengthens us.*" (Philippians 4:13)

**Consider:** What obstacles exist in your church, youth group or organization? In you? How can you overcome these?

# 9

# ~~What's~~ Who's in a Name?

*"Meanwhile, a group of people arrived to see Him, bringing*
*with them a paralytic, carried by four men".*

★☆  ★☆★

~

*In our 21st-century ministry called Capernaum we are attempting to see kids restored, just like the paralytic in the story. It happened in Capernaum.*

~

*"When He re-entered Capernaum some days later a rumor spread that He was at somebody's house. Such a large crowd had collected that while He was giving them His message it was impossible to get near the doorway.*

*"Meanwhile, a group of people arrived to see Him, bringing with them a paralytic, carried by four men. When they found it was impossible to get near Him because of the crowd, they removed the tiles from the roof over Jesus' head and let down the paralytic's bed through the opening. And when Jesus saw their faith, He said to the man on the bed, "My son, your sins are forgiven."*

*"But some of the scribes were sitting there silently asking themselves, 'Why does this man talk such blasphemy? Who can possibly forgive sins but God?'*

*"Jesus realized instantly what they were thinking and said to them, 'Why must you argue like this in your minds? Which is easier, to say to a paralyzed man, "Your sins are forgiven" or "Get up, pick up your bed and walk"? But to prove to you that the Son of Man has full authority to forgive sins on earth, I say to you – and here He spoke to the paralytic – "Get up, pick up your bed and go home."*

*"At once the man sprang to his feet, picked up his bed, and walked out in full view of them all. Everyone was amazed, praised God, and said, 'We've never seen anything like this before.'"*

(Mark 2:1-12)

Mary Ann, Kelly and I sat dejectedly in my office. It was March 4, 1986. The day before we'd made our third attempt to start our Capernaum Club. Like the previous attempts, the third was a failure. Our three false starts came after 18 months of research, planning, leasing a van once a week and securing start-up money given by the Kerley family. There we sat, three depressed and discouraged friends.

Mary Ann was my supervisor and my hero. When I initially came up with the idea, Mary Ann was my champion, so much so that when people saw her coming they knew she was going to talk to them about Capernaum. Meanwhile, my prospects as a future leader were bleak. Near the end of my training I knew I was going to be fired. The supervisors, except for Mary Ann, did not believe I could be a successful area director. She fought for me, kept me on staff, and told me she completely believed in me. She was my supervisor, but so much more! She was my cheerleader, teacher, spiritual mother and ministry partner.

After our third failure to start the Club, Mary Ann said, "Maybe this isn't meant to be. Maybe we just need to keep spending time with the kids, just being their friends." Kelly and I objected. "Let's give it one more try, we both said. "We are so close! Let's pray again."

That's when a thought came across my mind. "Hey, we're discouraged and it all feels so negative. Let's do something positive and give our ministry a name."

"OK, but what are we going to name it, Nicky?" Mary Ann asked.

"Capernaum Project."

I shared the story from the Bible that inspired the name. "I've been reading Mark 2:1-12, about those four guys with their disabled friend. There was no access to the house. They wanted to get their friend in front of Jesus but couldn't. They had to get creative and find a way. Someone came up with the idea of cutting a hole in the roof. They all agreed. It took four, maybe more people to get their friend on top of the house, but they wanted to get him in front of Jesus no matter what it took. It wasn't easy, just as we are discovering."

I continued. "So they cut a hole in the roof, increasing the cost of their friendship and knowing they'd have to pay for the damage, disrupting everything. Everyone was probably annoyed. Except Jesus. As they lowered him through the roof to Jesus, the Bible says Jesus saw **their** faith (not that of the paralytic).

My excitement bubbled over. "This story is about how much faith and relentless creativity we can have, not about the friends' faith – or lack of faith! The four friends were driven by their love for their friend. When you love and cherish someone, you do whatever it takes to help them. The cost doesn't matter. The four guys identified so deeply with their friend's plight, it became **their** plight.

"Then the plot thickens," I told Mary Ann and Kelly. "Jesus talked to the paralytic, seemingly completely missing the reason why the friends went to all that trouble. (They wanted Jesus to heal him.) But Jesus went further than the physical need. He told the paralytic, *Your sins are forgiven.* In the process, Jesus gave the man with a disability a backhanded compliment by forgiving his sins. Jesus calls him a sinner, putting him on equal footing with everyone in that room.

"But the Savior wasn't done. He healed him and restored him socially to the community. People were blown away! Just like people are going to be blown away when we get this ministry going!

"When we truly get what Jesus is doing and saying in this Capernaum story, we know that the disfigured appearance of the paralytic is a picture of our own sin-disfigured heart. All of us carry this sin disability within us. Jesus dealt with that condition before addressing this dear one's physical well-being. First things first, so to speak.

"Everything those guys did in the first-century town of Capernaum we are trying to do in our 20th-century ministry called

Capernaum. All of it. The failures, frustrations, hard work, creativity, and the needs for people, money, and other resources. We are attempting to see kids restored, just like the paralytic in the story. It happened in Capernaum!" I concluded, finishing my passionate soliloquy.

Our eyes brightened and we agreed to give it another shot, to give it our all, a fourth time. This time, though, with a new name and fresh understanding of the principles on which the ministry was built. That week, our very first Club was a total success!

I have seen the original, biblical Capernaum story repeated in our own Capernaum story thousands of times over the past 26 years:

- Four big-time football players helping a kid in a wheelchair get up a mountain.
- Leaders on duty 24/7 at camp, caring for their friends; feeding, bathing, bathrooming, helping them integrate into all the camp activities.
- Holding and hugging kids who go into seizures.
- Praying for and comforting kids' at their deathbeds.
- Women leaders doing a girls' makeover night.
- Helping kids get to their prom.
- Picking kids up weekly to go to a movie or a ballgame.
- Going out with a kid to grab a burger and feeding him while you feed yourself.

My favorite place in the world is the Grand Canyon, where I've visited and hiked many times. Four years ago we began holding one of our Capernaum weeks of camp at one of our Young Life properties situated just an hour from the Grand Canyon. That was when I got a great idea from God: Let's take kids to the Grand Canyon for a day! My excitement about the opportunity was tempered when I realized what it would take to get 200 kids with disabilities to the Grand Canyon without losing one over a cliff.

We planned for months. We thought through every safety and logistics issue involved in eating lunch there, bathroom stops, and handling the heat. We prayed about and thought through and discussed everything. By God's grace, those kids experienced God's majesty up close. None of these friends of ours had ever been to the Grand Canyon; most will probably never return. But it was worth it!

Our friends are very visual when they communicate, so we gave them the Grand Canyon - the biggest, most-beautiful, most out-of-this-world visual they had ever experienced. While there, we told them of a God so huge that this stunning canyon is tiny in comparison with its Creator. An incredible God, whose love even the Grand Canyon cannot contain.

Why go to all that trouble? Because, like the four Capernaum friends described in the Gospel of Mark, we are desperate and relentless to get our friends in front of Jesus. Those four friends wanted to go beyond feeling sorry for their friend with a disability. They wanted to make a difference in their friend's life. They wanted to walk their talk, so their friend could meet Jesus...and walk.

A few years ago I found out that Capernaum means "village of comfort." That made me smile, and wonder. From our three initial failures, a large village of kids with disabilities has sprung up across the world. It is a village where our friends experience the great comfort of belonging, self-esteem, purpose, hope and friendship.

**Consider:** Can you get some of your friends to take a kid with a disability on an impossible adventure?

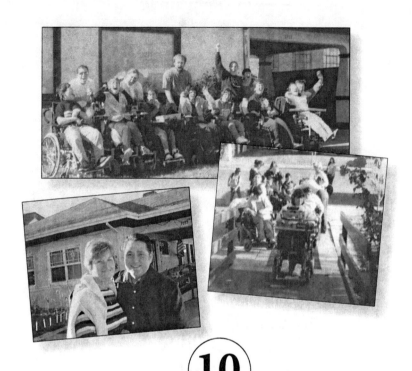

# It Takes a Village [called Capernaum]

*In 1986 there was one Young Life Capernaum ministry in the world. Today there are 210 in the U.S., along with Capernaum ministries in 28 countries!*

★☆ ★☆★

~

*Pray. Share the vision. Be tireless and relentless.*
*Be full of faith and know that*
*what you're fighting for is backed up*
*by the God of the universe.*
*Reaching kids with disabilities*
*is part of His agenda, and*
*He will accomplish it.*

~

In 1986 there was one Young Life Capernaum ministry in the world. Today there are 210 in the U.S., along with Capernaum ministries in 28 countries. The growth of Capernaum has been explosive and breathtaking, produced as the Holy Spirit has breathed power and special life into the people and prayers He chooses. We are simply along for the ride.

When I turned Antwon in his bed that night at camp, I discovered Jesus was right there too, disguised as a kid with a disability. Capernaum's growth began when I heard Jesus calling me through that young man.

After that, I asked others to join me. In time and with God's clear direction, we prayed boldly that the Holy Spirit would birth Capernaums all over the world. There was a great amount of disappointment, failure and learning during those times. But there was also faithfulness; people willing to stick it out over the long haul. Between 1986 and 1999, five Capernaum ministries launched. All were located west of the Mississippi. God was stretching me and enlarging my faith. In 1996 we celebrated 10 years of Capernaum in San Jose.

During that time my dear friend and intern, Julie, expressed her frustration with how she was doing ministry. She knew she was called to love and serve kids with disabilities, but not so much in the ways we were doing it. I told her that ministry – especially something as radically different as Capernaum – is like a blank canvas, on which people like her can paint their masterpiece. The edges of the artwork and the borders are Christ and the kids. Within those borders she could paint her ministry any way she wished. I told Julie to start dreaming how she'd like to paint her ministry masterpiece and share that with me.

The following week Julie came back with two pages of ideas about setting up a home for kids where we could hold Clubs, Bible studies, cooking classes, sleepovers, dances, and whatever else we could think of. I loved it! What was especially attractive about her dream was that we would be able to accommodate groups of kids in wheelchairs who couldn't gather in most homes because there just wasn't enough space.

When Julie finished showing me her vision for the kids, we both knew we had to go forward with it. As we talked about how to tell others so they would want to get on board, a very unlikely opportunity arose. In the final 30 seconds of our fund-raising banquet, while people were getting up from their tables, talking to one another, and getting ready to leave, Julie mentioned our dream of a house for the kids. I thought no one even heard her...until the next morning.

At 9 a.m., Carol Kerley called me. (Carol was on our advisory committee. She and her brother, Ken, and his wife, Alice, and their father, Joe, put up the first funds for Capernaum.) Carol said, "Nick I love the idea of a home for the kids. I am going to tell my dad to buy it. You go find a place, OK?" I couldn't believe my ears.

It was just one year later that we had our own Capernaum home, named in honor of Joe Kerley and his late, beloved wife, Ellie. From need to vision to a new home and new vistas for ministry, Joe & Ellie Kerley's Lighthouse is still blessing kids today.

Something huge happened. I saw how God does the extreme and impossible in quick order, with just our mustard seeds of faith. As the Lord dramatically enlarged my faith, vision and dreams, three verses became prominent in my life:

*"Now to Him who is able to do exceedingly abundantly beyond all you dare to ask or imagine."*        (Ephesians 3:20)

*"No eye has seen, no ear has heard all that God has prepared in the hearts of those who love Him."* (1 Corinthians 2:9)

*"Call to Me and I will show you great and mighty things which you do not know."* (Jeremiah 33:3)

Ministry growth begins when one person says, "Yes!" to God, praying hard while dreaming crazy and ridiculous dreams. From there, sometimes it means being naïve (trusting?) enough to believe God will answer. That's when the fun begins!

Two years later, my friend and fellow Capernaum teammate, Pete Cantu, decided to take a weekly prayer walk with me around the Lighthouse's neighborhood. We might have had a little too much coffee once in a while, but every week our walk started with us praying that Capernaum would receive a gift of a million dollars. We made a pact not to tell anyone. Eleven months later, someone I had met once for only a few seconds called me to say he was going to give Capernaum – you guessed it – a million dollars! In that moment I saw God's heart for our friends in a new way. I saw how big God's heart is and how He loves faith and dares us to go big with Him.

Shortly after that my phone began ringing nonstop. Young Life staff nationwide wanted to start Capernaum in their cities. Soon, they began visiting us in San Jose to learn how to do Capernaum ministry. As a result, we grew dramatically through a group of fellow pioneers who, like me, had no prior experience with people with disabilities.

A key to our strong growth was when a critical mass of ministries formed and we began to enter the mainstream culture of Young Life. Capernaum was like a parasite on its Young Life host, spreading the "Village of Comfort" virus to staff and volunteers throughout the organization. Young Life began to see disability ministry as an intricate part of its greater mission identity. This was a huge development and it was happening organically. No strategic plan, just Holy-Spirit-breathed, ground-up growth. The road bringing people with disabilities to the Lord's banquet table has been crowded with obstacles big and small. It took many years of faithfulness and patience for Capernaum to be accepted into the core of Young Life.

The encouragement to me and others beginning this kind of work is to stay the course. Pray. Share the vision. Be tireless and relentless. Be full of faith and know that what you're fighting for is backed up by the God of the universe. Reaching kids with disabilities is part of His agenda, and He will accomplish it.

A great example of this truth is Capernaum in the eastern U.S. For years I had prayed for Capernaum to gain a foothold in this area. One of our regional directors from Washington D.C. approached me shortly after he and his wife had given birth to a beautiful boy who had Down syndrome. He asked me to come to D.C. and talk to his region about Capernaum. Following that, two gifted women, Pam and Suzanne, began Capernaum in Washington D.C. and Baltimore. These represented the beginning of Capernaum's dramatic growth in the East and, eventually, the South.

Around this time, a woman named Zhanna, in Kazakhstan, had a dream for special-needs ministry that could reach people all over Asia. She contacted me and came to San Jose to spend time learning how to do Capernaum. When she returned to her country, she started Capernaum and it became our first international ministry. Soon thereafter, my friend, Walter, contacted me, ready to support us internationally with two $400,000 gifts.

Are you catching the growth pattern here? Completely organic, quick and abundant. Filled with life and led by fearless pioneers. As is usually the case, increased growth requires a solid infrastructure.

I recruited a national committee of men and women with hearts for kids with disabilities to help us with vision, support, and fundraising. I recruited an excellent administrator and a top-notch associate, both of whom complemented my gifts (and covered my weaknesses!). Then, we placed a Capernaum coordinator in each of our four divisions, to encourage existing ministry and foster new growth. Our leadership was through a team that balanced responsibilities for the organization's spiritual, financial and program needs, while encouraging complete freedom in which the Holy Spirit could operate. It has worked beautifully to this point and, hopefully, will continue into the future.

Capernaum's spiritual growth was just as dramatic. The kids, as well as the able-bodied kids, the volunteers, and the staff, were drawn more deeply into Christ and into our community of brokenness. Although many believed the kids couldn't "get it" because of intellectual and other disabilities, our friends were falling in love with Jesus. They were praying, serving and taking every opportunity to get more involved throughout the Young Life family. We began seeing kids serving at summer camp on work crews and as volunteer leaders. Some moved into positions with the Capernaum staff.

Our vision for the future is to serve the church by offering all we've learned to help the Body of Christ serve some of the millions of kids worldwide who have disabilities. The Master's banquet won't start until kids with disabilities are visible in our gatherings, sitting at the table hosted by Jesus. Jesus says His house must be full and the host in the parable says this too, right after he commands his servants to bring in the crippled, the lame, the blind, and the poor.

Come on friend, we've got some inviting to do!

**Consider:** What ridiculous dream do you have for kids with disabilities in your city?

# Mavericks Wanted

*We need leaders who will leverage
their biblical authority to help
lead our friends to take their full and
God-given seat at the table of fellowship.*

~

Maverick: *Someone who refuses to play by the rules. He/she isn't scared to cross the line of conformity. Their unorthodox tactics get results.*

(The Urban Dictionary)

~

When I joined the Young Life staff in 1983, one of our requirements was to attend the Young Life Institute. The intensive training combined theology courses with field courses in Young Life ministry work.

By then I had known my disabled friends for three years and had a lot of questions: Would Young Life accept this ministry? If I went after my ministry dream full-bore, how could I pull it off, particularly transporting kids in wheelchairs? It was all new, with no road map or handbook. As I sat in my first class at the institute I was praying and thinking about my idea of a full-on ministry for kids with disabilities.

Our first class, titled "Foundations in Young Life," was opened by the president of Young Life, Bob "Mitch" Mitchell. Mitch was Young Life Founder Jim Rayburn's first Club kid, so he had watched Young Life for 42 years from a front-row seat. As he shared with us a beautiful story of how God had miraculously and wonderfully worked in Young Life, something he said grabbed me. It was a powerful moment, a laser-sharp turning point in my thinking about a ministry to kids with disabilities.

"What we need today are mavericks" Mitch said. "We need people who aren't afraid to try something radical and, possibly, fail. Rayburn always said 'The best Young Life work is yet to be done!' and I believe that."

His words were like 10-pound raindrops drumming into my head. In my spirit I knew the Lord was telling me, "Go for it!!" Even if I didn't have all the answers, I was called to step out in faith, like the four friends who brought their paralyzed friend to Jesus, with no idea about how to get him in front of the Savior.

I knew it would take this type of maverick spirit to ignite and sustain Capernaum's kind of ministry. It meant shedding small-mindedness. It meant refusing to say "No" to kids with disabilities and their families, replacing it with, "What else can we do?" and "How could we pull this off?"

What does it look like when a maverick gets involved with kids who have disabilities? Glad you asked! I'd describe it as kind of a "Star Trek" state of mind. You know, a readiness to "Boldly go where no man or woman has gone before." It's asking God for new eyes to see and the courage to move forward into what is completely uncertain terrain.

That kind of approach toward what is new and challenging is really captured in the words of four of my heroes, John F. Kennedy, Bobby Kennedy, Condoleezza Rice, and Martin Luther King Jr.

> *"The torch is being passed to a new generation in search of a new frontier."*　　　　　John F. Kennedy

> *"Some men see things as they are and say, 'Why?' I see things that aren't and say, 'Why not?'"*　　　　Bobby Kennedy

> *"Victory always emerges out of darkness."*
> 　　　　　　　　　　　　　Condoleezza Rice
> *"I have a dream...."*
>
> 　　　　　　　　　　Martin Luther King

It's significant that these statements all reflect what we discover in Hebrews 11:1 - *"Now faith is being sure of what we hope for and certain of what we do not see."*

On the night before Dr. King was assassinated, he said, "The Lord has allowed me to go to the mountaintop. I have seen the promised land. I may not get there, but we as a people will get to the promised land." The fruit from his impossible dream has been abundant, the result of him looking past what is, to what could be.

One day I picked up a new kid for Club. It was Doug's first time and when he asked where we were going and I replied, "To my house," he shot back, "No we aren't."

"Yes, we are."

"No, we aren't."

"Doug, why are you having such a hard time believing that you are coming to my house?" I asked.

"Because no one invites us to their homes. They don't have ramps."

"My house does."

After a little bit of silence Doug said, "You really do want us there, don't you?"

Something you quickly discover if you are in a wheelchair is that our culture is rarely hospitable to people with disabilities. Faced with that reality, mavericks help create welcoming places for our friends with disabilities. They ask questions such as, "Is my house accessible? Does my church have ramps and accessible bathrooms? Actually, is our entire campus accessible?" Accessibility is an attitude that says "Welcome! We're glad you're here!" By the way, our welcoming attitude and accessible facilities benefit more than those with disabilities; it shows hospitality to everyone.

This approach may not seem very radical until you realize that many of the buildings in our communities, cities and nation are still inaccessible. Here's a maverick approach: Put up a ramp before someone needs it! That kind of proactive and prophetic action believes accessibility will lead to hospitality. And, to ministry opportunities.

More than one pastor has asked me why we should invest so much money and effort in so few people. Or, in some cases, in no people at all? To which I reply, "Why should Christ have died when so few have responded?" God's economics can make little sense to us. Why should the precious blood of the Maker of the universe be poured out for an ungrateful humanity? Christ's sacrifice was for everyone, though few might take advantage of it. I have often heard, "If you were the only person ever created, Christ still would have come and died for you." It's this belief and orientation that allows Capernaum to be what some might consider extravagant - for that one person with a disability.

But we've got to go beyond wheelchair ramps and ADA-approved restrooms. Our friends not only need access to our buildings, but into our very lives. This means initiating and nurturing relationships. The kind of friendships where we become vulnerable enough to let them into our busy, messy lives. Vulnerable enough to allow them to minister to us.

It's not about programs. People with disabilities are very familiar with the kinds of safe and impersonal programs that come and go (but mostly go). It's in-person, dependable friendships that matter. Ask any parent of a young person with a disability what they want most for their child and you'll probably hear the same answer: "I want my son or daughter to have a friend."

Once a fellow leader, Leslie, and I took one of our Club kids named Karen out for ice cream. When we brought her back home, her mother answered the door and told us to wait a minute. She returned with her purse and tried to give us $50. I said, "What's this for?" She said she wanted to pay us to start taking her daughter out once a month. I quickly protested. "No! We want to take your daughter out because we are friends with her."

Friendships with people who happen to have disabilities are cutting-edge and risky. Through these special friendships I learn about my friends' hopes, dreams, and shared challenges, which teach me how to more creatively and effectively meet their needs.

For Capernaum, one of those needs was setting up a place kids with disabilities could call their own and build relationships. As we began getting the house ready for our friends, they started asking questions like, "Will it have a refrigerator? Can I have food there? Can I bring a date with me?" The Lighthouse would be something that belonged to them, that they could enjoy with their friends. Modifying the house we purchased was very expensive, but we were OK with that. We were willing to do whatever it took to get even one kid to the feet of Jesus.

Maverick leaders in special-needs ministries respect and care for our friends so much, they believe in their kids' spiritual gifts and abilities. With this kind of belief, they start creating service opportunities for our friends. Not surprisingly, this kind of leader may encounter hesitancy, objection, and, at times, rejection.

When Paul followed his calling to preach the Gospel to the Gentiles, he was met with hostility from fellow Jews. Even Jewish Christians. They believed that Gentiles were outside the favor of God. We all need to understand and stand firmly upon these words from Scripture:

*"The eye cannot say to the hand, 'I don't need you.' And the head cannot say to the foot, 'I don't need you.' No! Those parts of the body that seem weaker are really necessary. And the parts of the body we think are*

*less-deserving are the parts to which we give the most honor. We give special respect to the parts we want to hide. The more respectable parts of our body need no special care. But God put the body together and gave more honor to the parts that need it, so our body would not be divided. God wanted the different parts to care the same for each other. "*

(I Corinthians 12:21-25)

We need leaders who will leverage their biblical authority to help lead our friends to take their full and God-given seat at the table of fellowship. Here's the deal: Applying the biblical mandate means Christians must include everyone at Christ's banquet table including, no, **especially** people with disabilities. Everyone with this mindset who participates in a church body or parachurch organization is profoundly and forever changed.

Over the years, thousands of volunteers have found and served kids with disabilities, only to find out (to their surprise) that they were changed to a greater degree than the kids. Every day we who are able-bodied are gently confronted by our friends about our own disabilities, things such as a complaining spirit; always being in a hurry; talking too much; harsh and critical attitudes; and being conditional with our love.

In ministries like Capernaum, a kind of mutual discipleship develops, creating a beloved and deep community of brokenness. Indeed, forming a community that's visible to the larger culture is critical. The first-century church was known as a sanctuary for the dregs of society: the slaves, women, tax collectors, prostitutes, and other castoffs. Their community of care formed around these exiled outcasts and was known far and wide as the place to go if no one else would accept you.

What if our 21st-century churches and Christian ministries became known as the communities that take care of people with disabilities better than anyone else? What if our mavericks, innovators and creative people were committed to having people with disabilities in leadership, doing things we never thought possible? What if we were 20 years ahead of the culture, instead of 20 years behind?

At that same summertime Young Life Institute, I took a Gospel of Mark class from my friend, Les Comee. It was fabulous. He made us wrestle with a central question: What is the Gospel?

We need to ask because what seems obvious at first glance is not really so obvious. We students tracked what it meant for the disciples to grapple with a Gospel message radically different from their experience and expectations, a Gospel truth that led them to unexpected places of suffering and featured an unexpected style of leadership servanthood. The Gospel we discovered isn't static, but dynamic, active, and people-changing.

That class helped me recognize what had been taking place inside me for the previous three years I'd spent with my disabled friends. They were my mentors, leading me to see a Gospel much bigger and much more inclusive than I'd ever perceived. And you know what else? The real mavericks are my friends, those kids who formed me into the maverick I am today. Anyone who dares to "be comfortable with being uncomfortable" and enter into a relationship with these special people will be a maverick, too.

> **Consider:** As you learn from your new friends, see what
> maverick ideas form from your friendship. And then, go after
> those ideas!

$\left(\,12\,\right)$

# Camp Miracles

*When I took my friends with disabilities to camp,*
*I found a complete and multi-dimensional impact. Not only*
*in their lives, but in the lives of everyone at camp.*

~

*We have a powerful, long-term vision.*
*That hundreds of able-bodied kids will have this*
*transformative experience each year.*
*That as these students head into their adult lives*
*they will ask their churches,*
*"Why aren't our friends with disabilities here?"*
*That these able-bodied kids will become pioneers who*
*help integrate their friends into our churches.*

~

Pat stood by the Capernaum van with a bemused look on her face. I was loading her daughter, Lori, in the van before we headed out for our first week of summer camp with our friends with disabilities.

Lori's mom was staring at us. Finally I asked, "What, Pat? What's on your mind?" She replied, "I was just trying to think of when, in the last 20 years, I've had a night to myself. You know, I never have had a day or an evening without Lori. And certainly not an entire a week!"

Parents of children with special needs must provide round-the-clock physical care for their children. Single-parent homes, which are common, face even more pressure. If their kid's in a wheelchair, the parents may not even have adequate transportation for him or her. Add to that the fact that people aren't exactly lining up to volunteer so these parents can get a break. That's when summer camp began taking on an even greater meaning for me. It was not only ministry with the kids we brought to camp, but also with their parents.

I knew the power of going to a week of camp because I had done it so often with my able-bodied, teenage friends. By getting away from all the pressures at home and living with leaders who built deep friendships with them, they were freed to consider Jesus. I had seen thousands of lives changed over the years.

When I brought six of my friends in wheelchairs that first summer, they transformed the entire camp - property staff, assignment team, work crew (high school volunteers), summer staff (college volunteers), and the 300 able-bodied campers.

Nine months later, we at Capernaum had learned a lot from that first weekend camp experience when I turned Antwon. We were more prepared and knew how to prepare others to be with our kids. We were slowly getting better as we became closer to our friends and understood their needs in a greater way.

When we arrived at camp, one of our first encounters was with 15 gang kids from Phoenix. One morning their leader approached me and said, "Nick, last night my guys told me they wanted to go home because everyone is staring at them. But, after talking about it more they decided to stay because those kids in wheelchairs are the only ones who don't look at them weird."

Later in the day, when a couple of these big, tough kids suddenly appeared next to me, I thought my life was over. One said to me, "Hey dude, are you the guy here with those kids in the wheelchairs?" "Yes," I replied hesitantly. "Well, we were wondering if we could push them around and hang out with them." "Wow, guys," I replied, "that would be great!"

And so they hung out with us and did camp with our kids for the rest of the week! What a sight: huge, street-hardened gang members, being tender with kids in fragile bodies. One of the wonderful things about my friends with disabilities is their open-arms embrace of others. They don't have a fear factor when it comes to relationships. It doesn't matter if you are a big, bad gang kid or the president of the United States; kids with disabilities simply want to welcome you into their lives.

One day, I was standing in line at the camp's snack shack with my friend, Steve. He was small, fragile and in a wheelchair. Next to him was one of the Phoenix gang kids, covered in tattoos, staring silently at Steve. As Steve looked up and smiled, the tough guy said, "Hey bro, if anyone gives you a problem you tell me and I'll kill him!" I quickly intervened. "Hey, thanks for the offer, but we have a camp rule against killing." We laughed, but even now, many years later, I'm still not sure how sincere the laughter of Steve's new-found protector was.

Nevertheless, there's one thing I **am** sure about: all 15 of those gang kids gave their lives to Christ by the end of the week. My friends played a major role in those conversions. Because of their hours together that week of summer camp, those gang kids and our kids forged real friendships. They understood each other. Our friends' openness and acceptance was something brand new for the Phoenix kids. As a result of the friendships, both our kids with disabilities and the gang members opened up and became vulnerable like they never had before. God's ways are amazing!

The next year we took a 16-year-old girl, Julie, who had become disabled as a result of her fight with cancer. She had been extremely active and social before the cancer, but ended up in a wheelchair, attending a special-education class. To make matters worse, her friends started abandoning her during her struggle with cancer.

Almost all of our Club kids are born with their disability. But in a handful of cases we've had kids who were in car accidents, electrocuted or, like Julie, contracted cancer. A person's fall from their health and the world they've grown up in - to a new and scary world of disability - is shocking beyond words. It's like you or me being suddenly yanked out of our familiar neighborhood and dropped alone in the middle of a desolate, endless desert without another soul in sight. For our kids who became disabled after their childhood years, the enormity of their completely changed world brings anger, shock, and, depression.

After her first Club, Julie's mom called me and asked, "What did you do with my daughter?" I immediately became anxious.

"What do you mean?"

"She came home and, for the first time in two years, she smiled."

That holy moment would soon be followed by an entire holy week of summer camp for Julie. It took a truckload of equipment and a round-the-clock nurse in order to take Julie to a week of camp, but she had the greatest week of her life. She did everything there was to do.

Our week of camp ends with "Say So," when kids have the opportunity to talk about their decision to follow Jesus (if they've made that choice). A song is played and kids who want to profess their desire to follow Jesus stand up. Many kids over the years have had their lives authentically and dramatically changed during their week of camp, and are eager to tell others about their decision.

As a song played and about 100 kids stood up, the microphone was passed around and each kid made a short statement. Finally, the mic made it to the left side of the room where Julie sat in her big wheelchair. One of our leaders helped her raise her hand. Then Julie took the mic and in her halting, slurred speech she said, "My name... is...Julie...I want...to...follow...Jesus."

As I wiped my teary eyes, every kid stood and gave Julie – by now in tears herself – a standing ovation. Soon, a small army of kids surrounded her, loving and comforting her. I made my way over and listened to her as she simply repeated over and over, through her sobs, "I...am...so...glad...God...didn't...forget...me." Julie's life was changed that week. She was restored to Jesus, to hope and to belonging. But, she wasn't the only one - everyone at that camp was changed. None of us remained the same.

One of the ways we all changed was by experiencing what it meant to truly serve. For our friends to be at camp meant everyone needed to adapt and adjust...the schedule, the program, the camp.

For instance, when the group of athletic, competitive guys started playing volleyball opposite our noncompetitive, fragile kids.

I know youth leaders who think this will wreck the camp experience for their kids. They discover that the experience of servant hood and cooperation is much more memorable and character-building than simply competing to win a contest. Sometimes, one of my friends can shake a jaded, know-it-all youth leader to his or her core. You know the kind: a leader who's done it all, heard it all, thinks he's seen it all; a leader like...me!

Picture this: We were in our Club activity at camp, with 300 kids going wild. When it came time for the Club talk it was about the cross of Christ. I sat by my beloved friend, Sarita, who has Down syndrome. She can't speak, but she communicates with grunts and her own sounds.

There we were, hearing about the cross, but to my great shame, I was zoning out. I had heard this talk many times. I had *given* this talk many times. I was lukewarm to the message.

All of a sudden I was startled by Sarita poking me in the arm. She stood up with tears streaming down her face. She poked me again and then she poked each palm hard and pointed to heaven. She was passionately, urgently telling me Jesus had died for her and me. Once again, like with Antwon (the young man who God used to change my life with his request, "Nick, turn me"), I met Jesus. Sarita discipled me and taught me. Sarita confronted my spiritual apathy and pointed me to Jesus with tears of joy.

After camp, Sarita's mom, Delia, wrote me this letter. As you read, keep in mind that Delia is a Christian.

*Dear Nick,*

*For years I looked for a church that would accept Sarita and her friends who also had disabilities, and have a place especially for them. I could not find one. Then, I heard about Capernaum Project. It was everything I had dreamed of! Sarita and her friends have found a place to belong. <u>It was then that I knew there was a God</u>, because there was a church for my daughter.*

*Delia*

Capernaum Project is not a church, but for Delia we are the closest thing to one. Capernaum became a much-needed place of belonging for Sarita and her friends. The shocking thing for me is that it took Capernaum to convince Delia there is a God. Conversely, when parents of kids with disabilities can't find a place of belonging among Christians, John 3:16 becomes: For God so loved (*most of*) the world that He gave his only Son.

Over the years I've witnessed the overwhelming impact of our friends on able-bodied kids. I began to wonder what would happen if we dramatically upped the ante. What if we created a week of camp with 100 kids with disabilities, and 100 able-bodied kids and one hundred leaders, and we all went to camp to encounter Jesus together? Through one another? It would be a reverse-mainstream camp.

The typical youth camp has, maybe, a handful of kids with disabilities among the 300 to 400 campers. The kids with disabilities have to adjust to the standard summer-camp program and pace. In Capernaum Camp we bring able-bodied kids together with 100 to 200 kids with disabilities, re-creating camp around their needs. We adjust the program, tempo, schedule and speaker to make it all disability-friendly.

The Capernaum week was the result of 18 years of learning how – and why – we do camping with kids who have disabilities. We were able to step up to the greater challenge of a camping program because of the sheer numbers of kids with disabilities. An important piece is that Jesus was magnified even more through the large numbers of kids with disabilities. Love, joy, gentleness and service were multiplied through this unique community of kids with and without disabilities.

We have a powerful, long-term vision. That hundreds of able-bodied kids will have this transformative experience each year. That as these students head into their adult lives they will ask their churches, "Why aren't our friends with disabilities here?" That these able-bodied kids will become pioneers who help integrate their friends into our churches.

Kids with disabilities can be part of **any** camp or adventure we plan. It takes adjustments, good communication with parents and care providers, and some extra volunteers, but all of it is totally doable. When we take our friends to summer camp, everyone wins.

I encourage you to take this step - you can do it. When I first took kids to summer camp I had no experience and plenty of questions and fears. But I learned as I went and you can, too.

> **Consider:** Choose a kid with a disability who you can befriend. Over the next year, prepare and learn what it would take to bring your friend to camp. Then invite him/her and watch God work.

# 13

# The Bible Tells me So

*It was a life-changing moment when I read
and re-read the parable of the Great Banquet
in the Gospel of Luke.*

★☆ ★☆★

~

*Six hundred million people currently
with disabilities would make up the world's
third-largest nation (but would rank
No. 1 in homelessness and poverty).*

~

With God's corrective lenses finally and firmly in place, I realized that Jesus' reference to "the crippled, the lame, the blind, the poor" (Luke 14) was exactly what it sounded like. My eyes were open to the Scriptures in a new way. Before, I had a blind spot, a literal disability when it came to really understanding that Jesus' parable was talking about people with disabilities.

With new eyesight and a fresh mindset, I began searching the Bible to find out what God had to say about people with disabilities. What I found was shocking. Not only did my understanding of people with disabilities grow, but God's Word on the subject greatly enlarged my view of the Trinity.

My intention in this chapter isn't to present an exhaustive survey of the biblical record regarding people with disabilities, but to show how often and how powerfully the Scriptures speak on this topic. For those who are willing to listen and act on what they hear, Jesus says,

> "A bruised reed I will not break.
> A dimly burning wick, I will not extinguish."
> (Matthew 12:20)

I discovered what seems so obvious to me now: God the Father created kids with disabilities just like everyone else: in His image. Even better, Jesus came and died for those who were created in God's image, including those with disabilities! Scripture taught me that the Holy Spirit engages kids with disabilities in their spirits (more so than in their intellect) to minister God's truth and salvation. As I picked up on the Gospel references to disabilities I knew I shared a common blind spot with the entire Christian community throughout the world. Seventy percent of the chapters in the four Gospels refer to individuals or groups of people with disabilities. But I had missed it! Despite years of listening to sermons, participating in Bible studies and reading theological scholars, God's focus on disabilities was never made clear to me.

My biblical investigation revealed a Jesus who intentionally and actively seeks out people with disabilities. For instance, at the pool of Bethesda (John 5), Jesus deliberately walked into a large community of people with disabilities and engaged them in a powerful, life-changing way. He could have completely avoided these special people, but chose to get close to them.

Remember the guy who approached my ministry booth (see Ch. 7), concluding there wasn't much of a market for a ministry like Capernaum? I think it's safe to say Jesus wouldn't have agreed. Christ made people with disabilities a major priority. He looked for, found, talked with and healed them. He ignored their so-called market value and focused on their Kingdom value. He saw them as wonderful creations of God, not statistics or sources of revenue that could improve His ministry numbers. Jesus thinks people with disabilities are so important He made them a major part of His ministry.

Is your response to that statement, "Come on. Really?" Well, you'll find the proof in that 70 percent of the four Gospels include references to disabilities. Beyond the sheer volume of Scripture about people with disabilities, notice the ways Jesus views and treats people with disabilities. When we study His message and manner, we see the value He places on these friends of His. (And we see how completely most of us have missed the heart of His ministry on earth).

Throughout the Gospels, Jesus affirms the dignity of people with disabilities and values them above man-made rules and traditions. More importantly, He repeatedly heals them in front of others and restores them to the community. Remember when Jesus healed the man with a withered hand, violating the Sabbath rules? The hemorrhaging and unclean woman Jesus had a one-on-one with as the crowd listened attentively? Or the leper He shouldn't have touched, but did anyway?

With Jesus, people came first, way before rules, religious traditions, or trying to gain the approval of those around Him. In Jesus, exiles and outcasts found acceptance, inclusion and belonging. Should we provide anything less when we encounter people with disabilities?

I constantly find other Christians who are unaware of the biblical mandate to include and love those with disabilities. Some people in Young Life, our churches and parachurch organizations tell me Capernaum's efforts are OK, but aren't really central to their ministry or to the overarching Kingdom work of all Christians. Really? Let me ask you a question. If ministry to the disabled isn't at the heart of authentic ministry, why did Jesus pursue it so frequently and effectively?

In Matthew we read the account of Jesus clearing the temple. This story is so important that all four Gospels include the account, emphasizing Jesus' anger at ministry becoming a marketplace. Of the four, though, Matthew gives us a stunning detail the other writers do not. In Matthew 21:14, after Jesus has torn up the place, we read: *"The blind and crippled people came to Jesus in the temple and He healed them."*

So, in addition to denouncing the ministry-marketplace activities and reminding His fellow Jews that the temple was intended for prayer, Jesus displayed His great anger toward the people and things that prevented people with disabilities from accessing His Father's house. Jesus, in fact, cleared the way into the temple for those who were excluded.

He got angry when people were mistreated. His passion for justice and for people burned when He found that His banquet table wasn't open to everyone. It only makes sense that when people were excluded from the temple, worship and life in the community, Christ would have been furious. In Jesus' ministry amongst people with disabilities He, like his cousin John the Baptist, was constantly preparing the way for people to get to God, helping them find community.

I saw this truth vividly displayed when I took my friend, Mike Flores, to Malibu (one of the Young Life camps). Mike had muscular dystrophy and got around in a big, old wheelchair. When we got to camp we discovered the grounds were divided in the middle, with an upper section and a lower section, connected by stairs. Mike approached the lower section with a crestfallen face, knowing he'd never be able to experience the other section of camp.

But the property staff saw the problem and quickly built a ramp. When it was finished, Mike wheeled over to me with his eyes sparkling. Speaking softly, he leaned over and said, "Nick, they really do want us here!" Then he was off to the lower half of camp.

What had been an obstacle became an opportunity. Not only for Mike to have access to the rest of camp, but for the able-bodied staff to learn the deep satisfaction of serving like Jesus served. A way had been prepared and Mike gained access to the community of kids at camp. He was included. He belonged.

When Jesus gives us His mission and purpose statement in Luke 4, He quotes Isaiah:

*"The Lord has put his Spirit in Me because He anointed*
*Me to preach good tidings to the poor. He has sent Me*
*to proclaim release to the captives, and recovering of sight*
*to the blind, to set at liberty them that are bruised."*
(Luke 4:18)

Jesus is not only talking directly about disability, He lives out His ministry purpose by choosing to be among people with disabilities. Over and over and over.

As John the Baptist languished in prison he began to sink into doubt and despair. Was he wrong about Jesus? Had John's ministry been a waste? Confused and discouraged, he sent his followers to question Jesus. *"Are you the one who is to come or should we wait for someone else?"* (Luke 7:19) What John had proclaimed so passionately and confidently was being eroded in a dark prison cell.

Jesus lovingly responded with these words of encouragement,

*"Go tell John what you saw and heard here. The blind*
*can see, the crippled can walk, and people with skin*
*diseases are healed. The deaf can hear, the dead are*
*raised to life and the Good News is preached to the poor."*
(Luke 7:22)

Strikingly, Jesus defines His ministry almost exclusively in terms of disability. It's not that Jesus doesn't care for all people, but His special emphasis seems aimed at the poor and broken. Those who know their dire need and are desperate for help. As Jesus said, it's not the healthy that need a doctor, but the sick. The truth is we are all sick, but only some of us know it and know enough to get help. Or, we know we're diseased but our pride or unbelief keeps us from asking for the help we need. Jesus is interested in the helpless, those who both know their condition and where to go and get it fixed.

Paul, describing the Body of Christ and sharing his concerns about how Christians treat one another, states, "*Those parts of the body that seem to be weaker are really necessary. And the parts of the body we think are less-deserving are the parts to which we give the most honor. We give special respect to the parts we want to hide.*"

(I Corinthians 12:22-23)

This so accurately describes our friends with disabilities, friends who need to be allowed to take their rightful places. What the world calls defective, God proclaims as key members of the Body of Christ!

Paul reminds us, "*But God chose the foolish things of the world to shame the wise and He chose the weak things of the world to shame the strong. He chose what the world thinks unimportant and what the world looks down on and thinks is nothing in order to destroy what the world thinks is important.*"      (I Corinthians 1:27-28)

We are pointed to the foolish, the weak, the unimportant and what the world looks down on as the place where we meet God. This flies directly in the face of pride, ambition, numbers and strength. Is this one of the reasons our churches fail to embrace those with disabilities? Could we be preoccupied with our culture's values instead of God's?

Sadly, that is exactly what we in the church have done. As long as we are content to worship at the altars of success, power, appearance and wealth, we will be numb, deaf and blind to people with disabilities. We need to hear the Old Testament prophets and their indictment of those who ignore and oppress the poor (in whatever form they appear) and kneel and wail in repentance. This may sound harsh, but if we choose to ignore the prophets and Jesus on this critical issue, we do so at our own peril. And loss.

The most important statement in the Old Testament regarding people with disabilities comes from Genesis 1:26-27: "*Then God said, 'Let Us make human beings in Our image and likeness.' So God created human beings in His image. In the image of God He created them. He created them male and female.*"

It should be painfully obvious, but many in our Christian subculture miss it completely. Human beings are created in **God's** image. Every one of us! Not some. Not most. **Every** human being. Disability does not nullify or hide the image of God as displayed in His creation. When we know and believe this, our view and treatment of someone with a disability changes radically.

This kind of major makeover in our thinking helps us become like David. 2 Samuel 9 contains my favorite story in the Old Testament. It's the story of King David honoring his friendship with Jonathan by bringing Jonathan's son, Mephibosheth, to Jerusalem to live with him and dine at his table, just like one of his own sons. Just one more detail: Mephibosheth had a disability.

Unlike most leaders in a culture like ours that prizes efficiency, David orders Ziba and 35 others to work year-round caring for and supporting Mephibosheth. The story ends with a reminder that Mephibosheth had two crippled feet. It comes across as almost comical. It's as if God leans over and whispers to us, *Hey, did you notice that My child, Mephibosheth, has a disability? But check it out – he's dining at the King's table! You know what? I really like Mephibosheth. Could you bring some more people like him to the table?*

Throughout the Old Testament we see God's red-hot heart for the poor and marginalized. The prophets constantly turn our attention to them, reminding us that God considers what many see as "the least" to be His treasures. Their value to the Lord finds its ultimate expression in the New Testament, when Jesus tells us in Matthew 25, *"What you have done for the least of these you have done for Me."*

A David leader seeks out people with disabilities. He ignores the cost or the limited numbers. He treats these men, women and children as royalty. A David leader helps transform their self-image, too. Instead of seeing themselves as dead dogs (that's how Mephibosheth saw himself) they are, instead, considered the king's sons, welcome at his banquet table.

There's a striking parallel to Luke 14:16-24 and the Great Banquet found in the Old Testament book of Micah:

*The Lord says at that time I will gather the crippled.*
*I will bring together those who were sent away,*
*those whom I caused to have trouble.*
*I will keep alive those who are crippled,*
*and I will make a strong nation of those who were sent away.*
*The Lord will be their King in Mt. Zion from now and forever.*

(Micah 4:6-7)

Let's assume that what Micah says is both true and is God's definitive word on the subject of those with disabilities. Let's also remember that the 600 million people currently with disabilities would make up the world's third-largest nation but would rank No. 1 in homelessness and poverty. What if God is sending out his servants - that would be you and me - to go to the "far country" described in the parable of the Great Banquet? Let's go out and find the crippled, the lame, the blind and the poor, as God begins to form a nation out of the rejects and throw-aways of this world.

The result would be a nation of belonging, purpose and joy for the outcasts who have known only exclusion and despair. In this new nation of the weak, I think God will most powerfully reveal Himself, shaming the strong. When we go out as His servants to find our friends with disabilities we get surprised. We realize that we – with our weaknesses, flaws and shortcomings – are being called with these friends to join them in forming a new nation under God.

> **Consider:** Do your own survey of the Scriptures for references to disabilities.

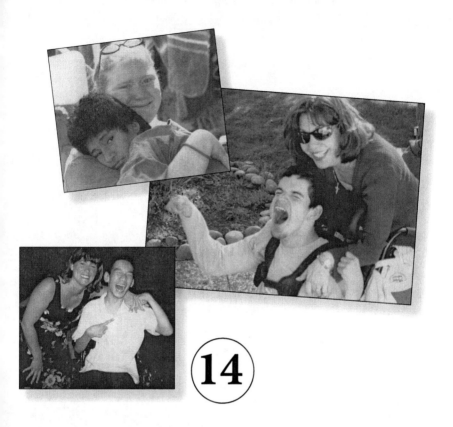

## 14

# Me? Disabled?

*"God's power is perfected in weak people, not in those who appear to have it all together. My friends and I hear Jesus say, "It is not the well who need a doctor; I have come for the sick." We love our doctor, our Savior, who makes house calls every day to help us disabled people!"*

~

*In a deeply broken world and despite their broken bodies, they display joy.*

~

I was feeding my friend Stashu a snack after a great Capernaum Club. Like many of our kids, he can't talk or care for any of his physical needs. But I wasn't thinking about that; my mind was on how lousy I felt.

For about six or seven years I had felt horrible. I wasn't sleeping well and even when I did finally fall asleep, I woke up multiple times during the night. Each day began with me feeling like I had to carry a 100-pound suitcase all day. My aches and pains distracted me so much I wasn't concentrating very well in conversations. My ailments made me start to dread going to Club and activities. But, between being an extrovert and prayer, I'd somehow rise to the occasion, only to feel horrible afterward. My doctor couldn't find anything wrong with me. I tried sleeping pills, but they didn't help. As I fed Stashu that evening, I thought about how horrible I felt and wondered how long I could continue to keep up the pace. I was frustrated and angry at life; and at God, who seemed remote and silent.

While raising Stashu's drink to his mouth and watching his lips slowly curl around his straw that evening, I looked intently into his eyes. I don't exactly know how to put this, so stay with me, but I saw Jesus during that moment.

I saw joy in the midst of suffering. In Stashu's eyes I found the humility required to receive help graciously. I sensed gratitude as I saw him attempting to reach out to me, while ignoring his own obvious and multiple needs. There was a sparkle in Stashu's eyes as I helped him with his drink.

Stashu experiences physical struggles every day of his life. He needs total care and is dependent on how well - or poorly - someone cares for him. He is nonverbal, so communication is frustrating because very few take the time to find out what he wants to get across to them. He's emotionally frustrated when people won't do what it takes to get to know him. I had spells of pain, but Stashu's suffering and limitations are 24/7. Yet there he was - smiling, with a sparkle in his eyes and in love with life. Hiding Jesus in his broken, unresponsive body.

It felt like Jesus, Stashu, and I were united in a holy, timeless moment. Stashu and Jesus were saying, "Nick, it's alright. I know. I know what it's like when your body won't work right and weariness overtakes you. I know about all of it, but you can still choose joy, even in the exhaustion and pain and lack of answers. I know."

I was being healed by Jesus through Stashu in that moment. But I also knew my healing was due to my attitude change toward my intense struggle with physical and emotional pains. Like Stashu, my physical struggle continued, but my friend led me to a place of acceptance, gratitude, and peace. He and Jesus did that, and I'm forever grateful.* The Lord had used my friends many times before to show me my disabilities, why should this be any different?

What are my disabilities? Two of them are my compulsion for busyness and constantly being in a hurry. When I am with my friends, however, I'm forced to slow down and focus on just one thing: being with them. I have to take time to really hear what a kid with slurred speech is saying. It may take a long time for her or him to complete even a few sentences. As my friends slow me down, I gradually relax and get to a place where I am calm.

Another of my disabilities is a lack of intuition. For instance, once when I was driving a few kids home in our van, Mary knew that her friend behind her in her wheelchair was having a silent seizure.

---

* Later, I was diagnosed with sleep apnea and my life has been given back to me through a CPAP machine.

Mary could not turn around in her own wheelchair to look, let alone help, but she knew what was going on. That's when I began to notice the ways my friends with disabilities looked out for and helped one another. Observing them, I learned how truly disabled I was. I am not nearly as intuitive about my relationships and can be unaware that someone needs help. Jesus just keeps showing up and revealing Himself to me.

Often I am very self-conscious when I'm in new situations with people I don't know. I do my best to try and make a good impression on them. I've learned, through friends like Paul, to relax and be more comfortable with others - and myself.

I met Paul when I brought some of my friends to watch a high-school baseball game. Paul is in a wheelchair. We had never met, but when he saw me he threw his arms wide open and said, "Hi, I am Paul. What's your name?"

"Um, Nick," I replied, disarmed by Paul's straightforward manner.

"Hey, Nick, it's my birthday on Saturday. Will you come to my party? And bring me a present?"

I laughed and was thinking about telling Paul that when you meet someone for the first time, you don't ask them to come to your birthday party, let alone urge them to bring you a gift. But then it hit me. Paul genuinely and totally received me, wanting to be open and trusting with me, his new friend. At the same time, I realized I was no different than him - I always want people to know it's my birthday and bring me a gift. Preferably an expensive one.

Paul was simply and powerfully expressing what I usually try to hide. Paul showed hospitality, openess and the ability to receive, despite living in a world that was typically cold, cynical, and rejecting.

In that moment I knew who the truly disabled person was…and it wasn't Paul.

Because of encounters like that, I began to see that kids with disabilities have a truckload of wisdom and God's love to show us. Those lessons made me want to expose everyone in Young Life to what I was learning and how I was changing. Probably the biggest realization was finding that we - the able-bodied but disabled in our own ways - are transformed as we draw near to kids with disabilities. Getting closer to these friends has helped me become more open with others, more thankful, more connected to friends. I was changing and it was about time.

Once I overheard two of our summer-staff girls talking at one of our camps. They had just finished spending a week with about 200 of our friends with disabilities. All week they had an up-close vantage point as they served, observed, and loved our friends. One said to the other, "They are on the outside what we are like on the inside. But they seem more whole on the inside."

I don't think anyone could have said it better. We all tend to hide our limitations and fears. Our disabilities, if you will. We don't want anyone to see us as anything but perfect, beautiful, articulate, charming, successful, (spiritual?) and sexy, so we wear a mask. My friends have no choice but to wear their disabilities on the outside. They have a genuine and mysterious acceptance of who they are, along with a lack of self-consciousness most of us cultivate almost obsessively.

I saw this the first time I took my friends to a movie. Throughout the film they carried on an out-loud dialogue with the actors! While I cringed in embarrassment, they were delighted. At a movie or anywhere else, they tend to say what they think and express what they feel, no matter what others think or feel about that freedom of expression.

Can that sometimes be a problem? Yes, so there are times when we help them with what is appropriate for the setting. Are they perfect? No, they are sinners like you and me. But in the midst of this they display a reality of the Gospel that we don't often see.

In a complaining world, they display gratitude.

While a man rants about the slow service at Radio Shack, my friend Kevin says, "Thanks Nick! Club is the greatest thing in my life."

In a deeply broken world and despite their broken bodies, they display joy.

While many athletes with near-perfect bodies grumble about their multi-million-dollar salaries, my friend Cesar with cerebral palsy says, "I am so happy we got to play football at school today!"

In a relationally cold world, they show warmth.

While being ignored by the Peet's coffee server (she's busy talking with her coworker), Big D rolls up to me in his wheelchair genuinely wanting to know how I am and how my week has gone.

In a world of human *do*ing they live as human *be*ings.

While most of us have a relentless drive to perform, my friend Katie (who is nonverbal and needs total care) sits at Club, taking it all in and smiling from start to finish, content just to be there.

In a culture that urges us to hide the truth about ourselves, my friends with disabilities display their true selves, encouraging onlookers to take it or leave it.

While I've often been a fake, hiding what I really feel to try and please others, my Venezuelan friend Gracie, who has Down syndrome, has no problem expressing her total anger at me for not remembering her birthday! And did she ever tell me!

In a broken and despairing world they display hope, despite the brokenness around them.

While I've been saddened by the depths of despair into which many able-bodied kids descend, pits deep and dark enough that some attempt suicide, I'm gladdened to hear my friend, Amy, who recovered from a near-death experience from a double grand-mal seizure, say, "Jesus had to let me go through this storm so He could show me He is with me, and can calm my storms."

I think what I love about my friends the most is their Christlike obsession with who I am as a person. Not what I do, or produce, or used to be, or might be someday.

In my job I tend to be measured by my performance. Despite the fact that it's a Christian ministry, I'm still evaluated and rewarded by larger numbers and bottom-line successes. For money raised and souls won. For speaking ability and charisma. When people who serve in churches and ministries are motivated by performance and/or fear, they become demoralized and are often abusive to one another.

My friends with disabilities shout out, "We are not what we produce or what we're afraid to reveal to others. We are children of God!"

My friends are like the suffering servant of Isaiah 53. We esteem them not and, in many circles, consider them the result of sin or tragedy. These so-called tragedies value me simply because I spend time with them. They really don't even care about how good Club was. They really don't care about how well I can do a Club talk. They absolutely do not care about my titles, degrees or successes. They care only about one title: Friend. That is success. That is what matters. It's in these sacred friendships that Jesus affirms each of us, accepting and using our disabilities and limitations to draw us to one another in community.

One of the most profound ways my friends have impacted me revolves around divorce. I've been divorced twice. I am now in a beautiful marriage of 23 years. But when my background comes up and somewhere in the conversation my being divorced is recalled, there is usually an uncomfortable moment. And, if people discover I've been divorced *twice*, the awkwardness is even greater. Especially around Christians. Many Christians believe those divorces disqualify me for leadership. I wonder what you thought about me when you read this paragraph.

Like most people, I would rather hide the truth of my marital failures. They're embarrassing, but true. Wonderfully, they're something my friends don't care about. I think another reason I like my friends so much is because we all have experienced multiple rejections and are fellow failures in this world. Not only do they not care about my successes, they don't care about my failures, either. I love that kind of unconditional acceptance! Just as they can't change their disability, I cannot change my divorces. Some people see us with a big, scarlet "D" on our foreheads.

Savor this poem by a lovely young girl, Marisa, who has autism.

*I am autistic.*

*I don't mind being different because*
*God loves me for who I am.*

*Sometimes people don't understand*
*I have feelings, so there is no reason to judge.*

*Everyone has a difference*
*so there is no reason to despair.*

*Even though I am still different*
*Jesus is still here for me*
*And those who come near.*

*Hand flapping, rocking, smiling*
*I am OK with who I am.*

*It makes me a better person and that is who I am.*

*I am glad the Lord made me*
*The way I am.*

*Being autistic is not that bad.*

*Having a difference is a blessing and*

*People should understand because*
*this is the way I am.*
*It is OK to be different because*
*God loves you for who you are.*
*So I am glad I am the way I am.*
*I am who I am.*

Me, Nick Palermo, disabled? Yes, like Marisa, I am. Thanks for helping me see myself through God's eyes. When I see who I really am, I find I'm completely accepted, disabilities and all.

> **Consider:** What are some of your disabilities? Do you attempt to hide them? Who accepts you despite your disabilities?

# "We're not set up for That Kind of Outreach"

*Sadly, one of the places where our friends encounter "No" most frequently is in the church.*

*Kids with disabilities force us to realize God is the
God of both the big and the small.*

"Is this something I will be able to depend on?"

The young man asking the question is Tyrone. He has cerebral palsy and is in a wheelchair. But the important thing to know is that when he asked that question he was 17 years old. His intellectual disability didn't keep him from being reflective and keenly insightful.

The "something" in his question was Capernaum. Would it be a place and community that would keep its word? Would it be something solid? Or, would it be yet another in a long line of disappointments? Tyrone remembered countless times when someone promised something, but didn't follow through. Pre-arranged transportation that never showed up. A much-liked program suddenly folding when funding was cut. Promised activities that disappeared from the calendar without an explanation or attempt at rescheduling.

"Yes Tyrone," I replied with a smile, "you can count on this."

I love the fact that Capernaum is a place where someone with a disability will hear "Yes!" instead of "No." A place of belonging, where she or he can begin to explore who they are, who God is, and where their dreams might take them. In most places, however, the first reply a person with a disability receives is "No." "No, you can't." "No, we won't."

Only about 10 percent of churches nationwide have a ministry for people with disabilities. The common thing Christian parents of children with disabilities hear is, "No, we don't have a place or a ministry for your child." It's the reason many stop going to church; Sunday schools are not equipped for welcoming children with disabilities. They visit church after church, hoping to hear the "Yes" that never comes. The next step for many of these parents is to question the priorities of God's people, even questioning God Himself.

Those churches in the 10 percent that are reaching out to people with disabilities are doing heroic things, like providing respite nights so parents can drop off their kids and get out for some rare and precious time for themselves. Some churches have fully integrated people with disabilities into their congregations. An army of volunteers is needed, but the payoff is huge. Trained volunteers go one on one with people to help with their physical needs, or like helping them open a Bible or hymnal. Or, they put on a prom so the kids can enjoy a magnificently prepared theme night and dance.

More churches are catching this vision and pooling their resources to provide respite nights for parents. Parents drop their kids off for a few hours and volunteers at the church care for and play with their kids. My own church has been doing this for the past several years.

After the first respite night we surveyed parents, asking them what they did with their gift of time. One parent said, "I went home and slept!" Unless you've been responsible for the full-time, 24/7 care of a child with a disability, you cannot fully understand the gratitude in this parent's statement. All of us parents understand what caring for a child involves. For parents of a child with special needs, however, the care never ends. It can be for a lifetime. On top of that is their concern about what will happen to their son or daughter when Mom or Dad dies. Imagine a parent's relief if they knew their church would step into the gap at that point and make sure the child had the care he or she needed after the parent was gone.

A second couple participating in the respite night went out on their first date in 16 years! We all get busy and can end up neglecting our mates and marriages but, once again, there is a difference for these parents. People don't line up for the opportunity to be with a child with a disability. Most of the time these parents must focus their energies on their needy child. A respite night can give these precious families relief, renewal and refreshment.

A few years ago we started a new ministry in Los Angeles. It really took off, as it usually does when parents get word of a dependable, exciting place for their children. A year after they held their first Club, I spoke at their fund-raising event. During the banquet, a parent spoke about her daughter's year-long experience going to Club. "When I picked my daughter up after her first Club, she was so excited! As we drove off she said, 'The leader tonight said Jesus knows my name!' Then she told us how her daughter made them go back to hear her leader tell her again that Jesus knew her name.

They had spent many years trying out churches, hoping to find one that would accept them. Not once did they find one that had a Jesus who knew her daughter's name. But at the very first Capernaum Club they found the Jesus who knew her daughter's name!

How is it possible for the church to celebrate and follow a Jesus that doesn't know a young person's name? The answer, of course, is that Jesus isn't like this; He knows everything about every one of us, including our names. Yet this parent's experience is common. When we say "No" to our friends with disabilities and refuse to do whatever it takes to welcome them into our churches, we inadvertently present a Jesus who doesn't know their name.

It doesn't have to be like this. A church can be big, while making sure the seemingly small and insignificant are cared for. Our ministries can perform and produce, but we can also let our so-called non-performing friends with disabilities remind us that performance and productivity are not our identity. Flashy, entertaining and excellent is fine, as long as we refuse to hide a group of nonverbal kids in wheelchairs who make loud sounds of unintelligible praise. As long as leaders insist that everyone worships together.

Why are churches often so inhospitable? Why do only 10 percent of the congregations in America choose to create a welcoming, accessible place for those with disabilities? I've got a few ideas.

The more the church embraces our culture, the more it takes on the culture's values. Over the past 30 years, hundreds of mega-churches have been established; their influence on the greater Christian community is not insignificant. They're big; they pay lots of attention to the numbers and can focus a great many resources on performance.

I'm not saying that a big church is a bad church, or that God isn't using the people and ministries in many mega-churches to expand His kingdom. It's just that when a church reflects the values that are prized by the culture, it tends to ignore the small, the insignificant, and the ordinary. Just because a church is huge doesn't guarantee God's blessing, any more than it does for a small congregation of 30. Kids with disabilities force us to realize God is the God of both the big and the small.

A disability ministry is not attractive. It takes way more resources to put up way smaller numbers. Everything moves slower and takes longer, and all that effort can appear insignificant to those who are geared to an ROI (return-on-investment) mentality that requires revenue and/or increasing numbers to justify its existence.

When we see Jesus singling out an outcast woman from the crowd and listening to her entire story while Jairus' daughter is dying, we see the Jesus of the less and the least. One needy, disabled person means everything to Him, even if it often doesn't to others.

Some Christians and churches take a very hardline stance on a person's intellectual ability to grasp the Gospel message as a qualification for conversion. This requirement creates a tremendous prejudice toward the person with an intellectual disability. Then the question, "Can they, do they, get it?" surfaces. Some churches refuse to offer those with disabilities baptism or communion, having concluded that because they don't comprehend or experience the Gospel message in the same way as able-bodied people, our friends cannot participate in receiving the Lord's sacraments.

Another issue is people's fear. Fear of the unknown – whether the source is things or people – is normal, but ignorance and fear must not dictate the ways we reach out to our fellow human beings. J.B. Phillips argues that real Christian faith charges full-speed ahead into the messy and uncomfortable. Paul reminds us, *"For God has not given us a spirit of fear but one of love, power, and discipline."*

(2 Timothy 1:7)

The No. 1 obstacle Christians and churches face, though, is the persistent attitude that says, "You come to us, to our buildings, to our programs," rather than, "Hey, church, let's stop waiting for them to show up here. Let's go out to where people are." Or, as one pastor told me, "Well, they are welcome here. They could come…if they wanted to."

But even when the church doors are open wide to the person with a disability, the Jesus they meet inside doesn't appear to know their name because the church is unprepared to welcome them. The churches that want to represent the Jesus who knows everyone's name will need an extreme attitude adjustment, as well as makeovers in its facilities, programs, and staffing.

Those adjustments and makeovers begin with a decision to start saying "No" to the word "No." Replacing the "No" with a "Yes" forces us to ask, "How can we do this? What will it take?" The best answers to those questions will come from the parents of the kids with disabilities. "What kind of support do you need? What would it take to give you and your daughter or son a great experience here at our church? Could you train us to be good caregivers for your child?

At the facilities and architecture level, we look around our churches and conduct an honest survey of the parking lot, doorways, bathrooms, sanctuary, meeting halls, and more. Here's a simple question, yet a church's answer to it can be mission- and vision-changing: What will it take to make our church a welcoming place?

A few weeks ago my friend Ruben took his family to a new church. Ruben has cerebral palsy and is in a wheelchair, as is one of his three daughters. The church's bathrooms were completely inaccessible, which Ruben pointed out to one of the leaders in his gracious, constructive manner. When he and his family returned a week later, the church had remodeled its bathrooms, making them completely accessible. You cannot imagine the message this sends to a person with a disability and what actions like these say about the Jesus in that church.

Organizations like Joni and Friends, Capernaum and a number of others want to create awareness and assist churches. The good news is that if a church really wants to be a place and a people that gladly receives those with disabilities, it can. The question is not can we, but will we.

If the Jesus in a church doesn't know disabled people's names, it could feel like this:

*I came to your church but there was no place for Me.*
*I asked for communion but you told Me I was not smart*
*enough to receive it.*

*I wanted to use the bathroom but My wheelchair wouldn't fit.*
*I waited for someone to talk to Me but your fears*
*overwhelmed your interest in getting to know Me.*
*I made involuntary noises and you asked Me to leave.*
*You never took the time to learn My name.*
*My name is Jesus.*

Or, we could be a different type of church:

*I came to your church and there was a ramp so I could enter*
*the building.*
*I rolled up the ramp and was greeted happily by a number of*
*people.*
*I tried to talk and even though you couldn't understand Me*
*very well, you kept trying.*
*You led Me to a classroom and introduced Me to someone*
*who would be my friend and help Me with what I needed.*
*You held a drink with a straw to My lips, and waited patiently*
*for Me to drink.*
*You began inviting Me to your activities and made sure to find*
*ways I could participate.*
*You read the Bible to Me and made jokes with Me. We laughed*
*together.*
*You took Me out to breakfast, and later on, to a movie.*
*But the best thing was when you invited Me into your home. I*
*took the bus to your house, rolled up to your door, came inside*
*and dined with you.*
*My name is Jesus.*

**Consider:** What would it take to make your church
a welcoming place?

# (16)

# Arriving at Withness

*"This week at camp I learned I am not a mistake, but a masterpiece of God."* — Audrey (with cerebral palsy)

~

*A "with-them," or withness ministry, turns
things in a very positive direction.
Being with kids, catching the spirit of Mark 10:45:
"For even the Son of Man did not come to be served,
but to serve, and to give His life as a ransom for many."*

~

What happens when churches and ministries catch the vision of ministering to our friends with disabilities? What does it look like and feel like?

While in Germany on our disability study trip, we sat with Rosal Stiefel, who had worked among people with disabilities for many years. Talking with us about her ministry philosophy of camps that includes young people with disabilities she said, "When we take kids to camp we go **with** them, not to them. We are on a level playing field, seeing eye to eye. We come together humbly, knowing we will encounter Christ together with each other and through one another."

I realized right away how profound her approach was when thinking about being with people with disabilities. When I conduct ministry as a "to-them" enterprise, I hold all the power, leaving my friend powerless. That kind of high-control mindset causes me to relate to them as projects, people who need my help, but don't have anything to offer in return. I can become condescending, they can become resentful and we both end up separated. No benefits for either of us. A lose-lose situation.

A "with-them," or withness ministry, turns things in a very positive direction. Being with kids, catching the spirit of Mark 10:45: *"For even the Son of Man did not come to be served, but to serve, and to give His life as a ransom for many."*

This same I-came-to-serve-not-be-served Jesus allowed a woman to pour perfume on Him and wipe her tears from His feet using her hair. Jesus' reaction? He commended her and pointed out that her service would be remembered for all time.

If Jesus both gave and received in ministry, why shouldn't I? I approach those I seek to serve with open hands, ready to receive Christ Jesus. When I am served by my friends with disabilities, it's a divine surprise because I'm used to being the one who gives, but doesn't receive. Christ's presence makes us both receivers and givers. In withness, we're all changed as we meet Christ in each other and with each other.

One of the most-powerful examples of this dynamic came from the story of a young woman I'll call Sharon. Sharon was an 18-year-old beauty and a friend of my eldest son, Joel. She attended our Young Life Club and was vivacious, talented, and always smiling. From our vantage point it looked like she had it all going on.

Near the end of her senior year she sent me a letter that truly shook me to my core, reminding me that disabilities are hidden in all of us. Outwardly beautiful, Sharon was a wreck inside - insecure, no self-esteem, sexually active, a regular user of drugs and alcohol. Her self-loathing and hopelessness were so severe, she had decided to take her own life.

Sharon's letter recounted for me the night she was in her room with a knife, preparing to commit suicide. As she sat on her bed that fateful evening, my son contacted her on Facebook. As they chatted she asked Joel, "Hey, what is your dad's job?" Joel, completely unaware of Sharon's crisis and plans to kill herself, described Capernaum and my role as its founder and director. Curious, she asked if we ever needed volunteers. "Sure!" Joel eagerly replied. "Why don't you come Thursday night and find out more?" "OK, I will be there," Sharon replied.

After their conversation, Sharon decided she couldn't commit suicide until going to Capernaum Club Thursday night; she knew she had to follow through on her promise.

Thursday night came and Sharon made her way to Club. As usual, Sharon was the outward picture of perfection, while filled with self-rejection on the inside. She wrote in her letter, "I entered the room hesitantly, expecting to feel the inner rejection I've always experienced everywhere else, whether in school or church. But I felt more accepted in the first 30 seconds from a room full of drooling kids in wheelchairs than I had anywhere else in my life."

In the letter, Sharon described how dramatically her life had changed since she visited that Club. She quit drugs and alcohol, and broke off the relationship with her boyfriend. She described how God became her true Father and that she wanted to serve Him for the rest of her life.

Sharon had walked in to find out how she could help poor, unfortunate, kids with disabilities, but ended up meeting Jesus instead! The Jesus who always accepted and affirmed women, and held them in the highest esteem. Like Mary Magdalene, Joanna, Susanna, and others, Sharon now followed Jesus with them.

Sharon is one example of thousands of able-bodied kids in Young Life who have discovered the withness experience and been completely surprised. Any of us, if we allow ourselves to find and follow the withness-ministry pathway, will discover a group of people who minister in miraculous, life-changing ways through the sacrament of brokenness. The church becomes complete when we acknowledge and embrace the parts of His Body that are so easily ignored.

We'll also find that hidden under the disguise of disability are spiritual gifts, abilities and talents, people who are ready to serve others. As we begin to discover our own disabilities we'll find that God can use them in ministry to others – perhaps even to those who've ministered to us. In Young Life Capernaum, kids move from being ministry recipients to ministry leaders, work crew, and staff.

The withness approach helps us need our friends with disabilities as much as they need us. Most importantly, we increasingly display the kingdom of God in our actions and attitudes. One thing God loves to see in His kingdom is difference and variety. Our friends bring unique strengths and more to the mix, but one thing really stands out to me, especially as our nation still wrestles with racial tensions.

Sometime during our first year I was enjoying a snack after Club with my friends. Lively conversations, music and joyful laughter filled the air. Leaders jostled with kids playfully, as the late-afternoon sunlight danced on our smiling faces. Taking it all in and feeling like the luckiest person in the world, I realized there was an ethnic smorgasbord around the room: Jermaine and Antwon, African-Americans; Paulette, Native American; Tommy and John, Mexican; and Ju, Asian. What's more, these kids had grown up together from age 2 to 22. They were in special-education classes together over the years and had become great friends.

They were racially reconciled through a most unlikely way – disability. Incredible! What our nation still struggles with so deeply – despite a multitude of brilliant minds, strong wills, education, money and resolve – my friends with disabilities did without ever giving it a thought. Those who our society pities and rejects achieved the community and harmony our nation can only dream about. Truly, God has chosen the foolish to shame the wise, the weak to shame the strong.

Each of us can intentionally take on an issue like racial inequality and come together, agreeing that our place in the community of Christ should not be limited by skin color or ethnicity. When this happens among us we become, in the words of singer Toby Mac, a "diverse-city." Diversity! And, a beautiful city set on a hill.

Finally, I want to encourage you. I wish for you what I have received by the grace of God and *I pray* that you'll take the risk of being comfortable with being uncomfortable.

*I pray* that you'll begin a friendship with one young person with a disability, and that he or she becomes one of your best friends, intricately woven into the fabric of your life, your family, your church, and your relationships.

*I pray* that in your new friend you will meet Jesus in a new, deeper and healing way.

*I pray* that your friendship will help you see and accept yourself as the wonderfully designed - and greatly disabled - person you are. And that when that happens you, like your friend, will realize God's greatest treasure comes in broken, ordinary clay pots.

God bless you! I'm headed out to a midnight movie with my best friend, Adán. He feels sorry for me because I can't get in first like he can, so he takes me as an attendant. Jesus was right – the first shall be last and the last shall be first.

## About Nick Palermo

Nick is the founder of Young Life Capernaum and currently serves as the Director of Metro Capernaum - Santa Clara Valley. He has served on Young Life staff for 29 years, including 13 years as National Director of Capernaum. He's not only passionate about his friendships with kids with disabilities, he loves his family, his church, and baseball. A hardcore Giants fan, he hopes someday to serve as a program vendor and "ball dude."

Nick and his wife, Sue, have been married 23 years and have three boys. He's earned his B. A. in sociology (San Jose State University) and his masters in Theology (Fuller Seminary).

## About Capernaum

Get more information about Capernaum, explore opportunities to be involved and more at:
Metro Capernaum - Santa Clara Valley
1123 Hanchett Ave., San Jose, CA 95126
408-286-3433
www.capernaumprojectsj.younglife.org

To purchase additional copies of "Missing Stars, Fallen Sparrows," please contact:
Goehner Publications
408-246-6002 or info@goehnergroup.com
The book is also available at www.amazon.com

A portion of each book sale will be donated to Young Life Capernaum – Metro Area, in San Jose, California.

In the words of Jesus, *"Whatever you did for one of the least of these brothers of mine, you did for Me."*

CPSIA information can be obtained at www.ICGtesting.com
Printed in the USA
LVOW12s0345190314

378016LV00001B/37/P